TAEKWONDO
Philosophy & Culture

KOREAN TRADITIONAL MARTIAL ART

TAEKWONDO
Philosophy & Culture

by
Kyong Myong Lee

HOLLYM
Elizabeth, NJ · Seoul

First publshed in 2001
by Hollym International Corp.
18 Donald Place, Elizabeth, NJ 07208, U.S.A.
Tel : (908)353-1655 Fax : (908)353-0255
http://www.hollym.com

Published simultaneously in Korea
by Hollym Corporation ; Publishers
13-13 Kwanchol-dong, Chongno-gu, seoul 110-111, Korea
Tel : (02)735-7551~4 Fax : (02)730-8192, 5149
http : www.hollym.co.kr

ISBN : 1-56591-157-1 (hardcover)
ISBN : 1-56591-163-6 (softcover)
Library of Congress Catalog Card Number : 00-106352

Printed in Korea

THE WORLD TAEWKONDO FEDERATION

635 YUKSAM-DONG, KANGNAM-KU, SEOUL, KOREA 135-080   TEL:(82-2) 566-2505, 557-5446 FAX:(82-2) 553-4728
Intermeet Server : http : //www.worldsport.com E-mail : wtf@unitel.co.kr

Taekwondo, originated in Korea 2000 years ago as the traditional martial art, has its population of 50 million practitioners in 160 countries throughout the world. It also has accomplished its international stage as one of the most modern popular sports, especially following its promotion to the official status of the Sydney Olympic Games this year, which will mark the turning point of its history.

The initial motives for entering into Taekwondo training lie in desire to maintain or improve healthy condition or self-defense skills. On the other hand, however, Taekwondo in its practice puts more essential values to promote mental qualities as a tool of philosophy of life such as concentration, self-control and bravery with aim to realize the humanity.

In a sense, Taekwondo has been making a major role required by the basic philosophic factors of Taekwondo training to the modern society with big influence of its morality to the youth.

The author of this book, Prof. Kyong Myong Lee, who has ever worked as a WTF Deputy Secretary General, had a wide range of the study and research in the field of

THE WORLD TAEWKONDO FEDERATION

635 YUKSAM-DONG, KANGNAM-KU, SEOUL, KOREA 135-080   TEL:(82-2) 566-2505, 557-5446 FAX:(82-2) 553-4728

Taekwondo techniques, training, Pumsae, and management of international Taekwondo events, etc, especially having renown for the study of philosophy of martial arts.

I believe that this book will provide all the Taekwonoins with the basic concept of Taekwondo *'What is Taekwondo philosophy?'*

December 2000

Dr. Un Yong Kim
President
The World Taekwondo Federation

Official Sport in Sydney 2000 Olympic Games

Grand Master Kyong Myong Lee

Master Lee, a Gukgiwon-authorized 9th-dan black-belter, has a licence of Qualification for Coaching issued by Austrian authority. He has served as a Deputy Secretary General of World Taekwondo Federation (1991~1999)
- Professor, Departament of Sports Diplomacy at Chungcheong College
- President, Taekwondo Culture Institute

● Major Career
- Vice President, Austria Taekwondo Association
- Chairman, Technical Committee of ATA
- Manager, Coach and Trainer, Austrian Taekwondo Teams
- Permanent Member, Test Committee for Polish Taekwondo Association
- Manager, Polish National Taekwondo Team
- Chairman, Technical Committee of European Taekwondo Union
- Mamber, WTF Technical Committee
- Coach, Austrian National Taekwondo Team for the 1988 Seoul Olympic
- Lecturer, National Academy for Coaches (Austria)

● Educational Background
- Yonsei University (B.A. Philosophical Science)
- Graduate Course of Yonsei University (Press and Public Relations)
- Honorary Doctorate, Lipetsk State Pedagogical Institute Russia

● Written Accomplishment
- Essays : Grounds of Cognition and Yearning
          Roving through the World
          The Way of a Philosophical Martial-art Man
- Texts : Richtig Taekwondo (Munich, 1987)
          Taekwondo (Warsaw, 1989)
          Taekwondo Kyorugi (Hartford, 1994)
          Dynamic Taekwondo (Seoul, New Jersey, 1995)
          Taekwondo (New York, 1996)
          Taekwondo Kyorugi (Seoul, 1996)
          Taekwondo Kyorugi (Warsaw, 1999)
          Dynamic Taekwondo Kyorugi (Seoul, New Jersey, 1996)
          A Modern Hirtorty of Taekwondo (Seoul, 1999)

Taekwondo is an international sport, and there is a growing interest in the development of increased concentration and spirit in many parts throughout the world. Taekwondo is one of the most popular worldwide martial arts and it contributes not only to the improvement of human health but also to the establishment of human unity within society.

For many years I have taught Taekwondo in Europe. I concentrated on Taekwondo philosophy with a special emphasis on teaching as well as researching Taekwondo. I feel a deep connection with the principles of Taekwondo. It is my vocation in life. I have been Deputy Secretary General of the World Taekwondo Federation and at present I am lecturing Taekwondo philosophy to College students.

This book is based on the contents, the research and teaching methods I have developed until now. I also include an outline of the development of the World Taekwondo Federation and other associated institutions. In addition, Taekwondo will also be introduced as an official event of the Olympic Games and this entry will be discussed and examined.

Taekwondo not only fortifies the body and spirit through physical exercise but it also contains 'Han' philosophy in every movement. This book highlights the connection between 'Han' philosophy and Taekwondo in order to improve Taekwondo culture.

This book is dedicated to all who have an interest and affection in Taekwondo. I am very happy that my text on 'Taekwondo Culture and Philosophy' is being published by Hollym. My first two works being published by Hollym publishing were 'Dynamic Taekwondo' and 'Dynamic Taekwondo Kyorugi'. Any advice from readers concerning those texts and the philosophy of Taekwondo will be sincerely appreciated.

Finally, I want to express gratitude to the editor Ms. Julie Han and the president of Hollym publishing Mr. Ki-Man Ham without whom this book would not have been possible.

December 2000

Kyong Myong Lee

CONTENTS

Chaper 1 One

Taekwondo and Korean Culture

1

Taekwondo and Korean Culture

Taekwondo is a traditional cultural heritage of Korea. It started from ancient martial arts of Korea and has now grown to become an international sport, finally attaining its inclusion in the official program of Sydney 2000 Olympic Games.

The term taekwondo comes from a compound of *taekwon* and *do*. *Taekwon* is a symbolic expression meaning a system of offense and defense techniques exercised by the members of a human being, i.e., arms and legs. On the other hand, the word *do* was once mentioned by a modern Korean scholar Choi Chi-won, who described, in his *Prologue of Nallang Monument*, that our country has an occult *do* which can be analogized with *pungryu* (elegant arts). Therefore, the philosophical nature of *do* may be sounded out from Choi's expression of occult *do*. In short, *taekwon* means a system of physical techniques while *do* a system of metaphysical philosophy.

Korea's traditional culture has been formed on the basis of the philosophy of *Han* or *triple taegeuk,* representing heaven, earth, and human being, and also the philosophy of yin-yang and the five elements of the universe (metal, wood, water, fire, and earth). In other words, Korean culture was rooted in the *Han* philosophy. This phoneme *han* forms a great variety of compound words in the Korean language, namely, *Hangeul* (the Korean alphabet), *hanbok* (Korean costume), *Hanminjok* (Korean race), *hanji* (traditional Korean paper), and many others. There is also an emblem of tricolor *taegeuk* called *samtaegeuk* habitually used in the daily life of the Korean people, which signifies the three essentials of the universe, i.e., heaven, earth, and human being. One can easily find in Korea the emblem of *samtaegeuk* on the gates of shrines and temples, Korean musical instruments such as *buk* and *janggo*, paper fans, various monuments and pavilions, and even on the gates of royal tombs, stone stairways of the Royal Palace and temples, which are the most typical symbols of Korea.

The word *han* literally means one, many, same, middle, about, and others, containing in all 22 different meanings. The Korean people founded a nation on the basis of this ideology of *Han* or *taegeuk*. They believed that yang and yin represented the sky and the earth respectively, and that the human being mastered the little universe consisting of the five elements of the universe. For the Orientals, the human being is identical to the universe; for, they believe the cycling, movement, and mutuality of the universe correspond with those of human beings. Thus, the human being as the little universe is a real existence acting in accordance with the principles of *taegeuk* philosophy or yin-yang and five elements of the universe. *Taeguk* means the original condition of the universe at the time of its creation. Then, *taegeuk* evolved into two counterparts of yin and yang. A theoretical analysis of *taegeuk* contains the reasoning of how the universe was created.

Now, as to taekwondo, we can assume that it originated in ancient times along with the emergence of the Korean race and has been developing throughout all the evolution of the Korean people. Today, taekwondo is a martial arts sport, ever growing as a reputed international sport characteristic of its typical tastes of Korea as well as its nature of universality. The *Han* philosophy and yin-yang principles are well manifested not only in the system of taekwondo techniques but in the taekwondo costume (*dobok* and girdle), which are all related to the philosophy of *taegeuk*.

The Korean national flag represents the *taegeuk* philosophy. At the center of the flag something looks like revolving with two different colors, red and blue, on a white ground. The circle at the center symbolizes *taegeuk* and the 4 symbols of *gwe* (combination of divination signs) at 4 corners of the flag represent heaven, earth, water, and fire, respectively. That is to say, the *taegeuk* flag symbolizes yin-yang and the 4 elements of the universe, the white color as a ground representing the source of light, which is the basis of 5 different colors. The name of Baedal Race, the ancient Korean race, was derived from that white color.

Likewise, the taekwondo costume or *dobok* is unified to be of white color, and the *dobok* girdles are classified into 5 different colors, i.e., blue, yellow, red, white, and black, which signify the 5 elements of the universe. Even the United Nations recognizes the pattern of *taegeuk*, the proper design of Korea, and uses the mark of *taegeuk* design as a symbol of peace. In the same way, taekwondo techniques also have been developed on the basis of the *Han* philosophy, which is the proper Korean national thought. Therefore, all taekwondo pumsaes (sets of movements for taekwondo arts), beginning with Pumsae Taegeuk and ending with Pumsae Ilyo, have a connection with the principles of *Han* philosophy.

The *Han* philosophy is believed to be characteristic of non-Archean creation, and therefore this special quality of *Han* has served as the driving force for the Korean race to sustain itself positively throughout all the history of mankind. That is because the *Han* philosophy seeks peace instead of war and harmony rather than conflict. As a traditional culture of Korea, taekwondo, indeed, has long inspired the Korean people with the national spirit of *Han* philosophy, through the maintenance of various forms of martial art systems descending from ancient times, such as the Koguryo Kingdoms *jouiseonin* and the Silla Kingdoms *hwarang-do* or *pungryu-do*. Now that taekwondo, an outstanding token of Korean culture, has become an Olympic sport, it is sure that it will not only help promote the health of mankind but maintain peace in the whole world, just as it is pursued by the Olympic Movement.

Taekwondo has been included in the list of items to represent the corporate identity (CI) of Korean culture. It really deserves the title as a traditional culture of the Korean people because it is the martial arts consisting of all technical movements constructed on the basis of the metaphysical thinking and philosophical principles of the *Han* philosophy. Taekwondo is also called a martial art sport because it is now a globalized sport inherited from traditional martial arts of Korea. The global propagation of taekwondo is aimed at attaining a universal dissemination of the most typical tradition of Korean culture because it eyes achieving ultimately a universal globalism through an exquisite harmony of modernism with tradition, the view of individual values with the view of world values, the spirit with techniques, and martial arts with sports.

Chaper 2 Two

History of Taekwondo

2

History of Taekwondo

The Root of the Korean National Martial Arts

Man is endowed with the instincts to protect or defend himself and to preserve his own tribe. These instincts naturally made people perform physical activities, conscious or unconscious, and then bare-handed fighting techniques and defensive martial arts were to be developed as their living environment required. In fact, it is difficult to precisely trace back to the origins of the Korean martial arts. However, tradition says the martial arts of the *Han* (Korean) race was once called Dongi martial arts founded by the Dong-i race. There is no doubt that the Dongi race was an equivalent to the Baedal race, an ancient name of the Korean race. It can be assumed that there existed a certain form of national martial arts even prior to the Old Choson period according to some historical records of the pre-Old Joseon era, such as the *Handan-gogi* (old records) and the *Gyuwon-sahwa* (historical tales), in which famous warriors like Unsa and Chiu Cheonwang were frequently mentioned about. An authentic historical research of the proper Korean martial arts which was prevailing in the Three Kingdoms period was first attempted by a group of Japanese, who made trips of field investigation to study the historic sites of the Goguryeo Kingdom three times in 1910, 1935, and 1937. The exploration team visited the Tonggu area in Manchuria, China, where the ancient capital of Goguryeo was situated, and found there old tombs belonging to the Goguryeo Kingdom. There were mural paintings inside some of the tombs: a painting of warriors in the Samsil Tomb presumably built around the 5th century; a painting of gyeorugi (one-on-one fighting) in the Muyong Tomb presumably built around the 4th century; and a painting of *ssireum* (Korean-style wrestling) in the Gakjeo Tomb. All these paintings vividly displayed old forms of the Korean martial arts. Especially, the painting of gyeorugi excavated at the Muyong Tomb fairly well depicted an energetic image of two warriors in a stance of one-on-one fighting. Documentary records tell us various stories about the proper national martial arts descending down from the Three-Kingdoms era. Of course, the traditional martial arts were named differently according to the time and place, such as *subak*, *subyeokta*, *gukseondo*, *taekgyeon*, and *subakhui*, although most of the denominations have been transmitted to the modern Joseon Age.

Historical records of *the Samguk-sagi* and *the Goguryeo-bongi* explained that the play of *subak* was popular and groups of warriors called *jouiseonin* were organized in the days of Goguryeo. Also, a maritime record of *the Haesang-japnok* carried a story about Kaesomun, who was described as coming from the group of *jouiseonin* (or *seonbae*). The people of the Baekje Kingdom called their martial arts *subyeokta*. Referring to this martial arts, a historical record of *the Haedong-ungi* described that we have old practices of hand arts which use hands as if using a sword. General Cheok adopted the hand arts to teach soldiers. If at all one hand fails to follow the rule in the midst of exchanging the strokes of two hands, ones head will fall down in a wink.

Martial arts of the Silla Kingdom may be well explained by the system of Hwarangdo training. King Jinheung of Silla is known to have introduced from Goguryeo the *seonbae* system to strengthen his kingdoms youth organization called *pungryudo* or *pungwoldo*. However, Silla developed its own martial arts called *taekgyeonsul*, usually called *subak* or *subyok* or *taekgyeon*. A royal record of *the Jewang-ungi* narrated a story about the *taekgyeonsul*, saying Among the old customs of Silla there was a play of *bigaksul* (foot-flying arts) with which two competitors confronted each other to kick down the opponent. There were three levels of techniques: some could kick the opponents legs only, while others could kick the opponents shoulders; yet, some most skilled fighters could kick the hair topknot on the opponents head, which was called *bigaksul*.

The fact that Sillas *hwarangs* (youth elite), who played a great role in achieving unification of the Korean Peninsula under the rein of Silla Kingdom, practiced old martial arts, can be easily attested by various historical monuments in Gyeongju, the ancient capital of Silla; for example, Geumgang warriors statues at Seokguram and copper statues of Geumgang warriors at Gyeongju Museum, whose stances vividly exhibit offense and defense postures.

Coming down to the Goryeo era, martial arts called *subakhui* was popular according to the *History of Goryeo*, which said that the king was watching *subakhui* contests while staying at a pavilion and the king proceeded to the Hwabi Palace to watch *subakhui* contests and the like. It seems that kings of Goryeo were much interested in *subakhui* because it was a compulsory subject of training for all soldiers. Those soldiers who were well skilled in *subakhui* could enjoy a special promotion. *The History of Goryeo* also stated that Lee Ui-min and Du Kyong-sung were competing with each other, boasting of their skill of *subakhui* by demonstrating their strength: Lee hit a pillar of a house with his fist to make roof-supporting rafters felt shaking, and Du punched the wall with the fist to make it pierce through the wall. Therefore, the level of martial arts skill in the Goryeo era was so high that its power and techniques could even deliver a fatal blow to an opponent. The Goryeo dynasty even adopted a training method of group combat under the name of five-soldier *subakhui*.

In the Joseon Age, there were various types of martial arts under different names, such as *taekgyeon*, *taekgyeonhui*, *subyeok*, *gwonbop*, and others. It is said, in the *Taejong Sillok* (True Records of King Taejong), that the government agency Uihungbu in the 10th year of Taejong (1410) adopted a *subakhui* test for the recruitment of soldiers, assigning the passers of the test to the defense troop. Also, the *Sejong sillok* described that village servants or official servants of Damyang County rallied to the training of *subakhui*, hearing a news that the government was recruiting soldiers by the test of abilities in *subakhui*. These records show that, like in the Goryeo Age, the Joseon dynasty, too, adopted the *subak* martial arts as a test subject for recruiting soldiers.

Transmission of Traditional Korean Martial Arts

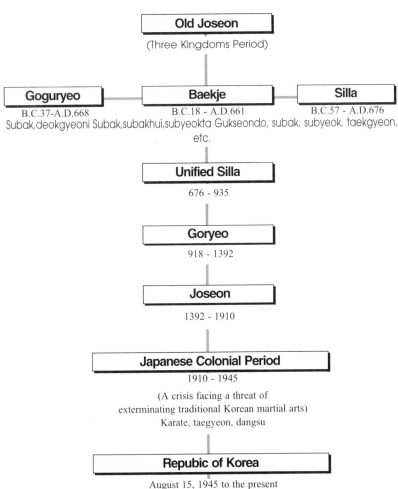

Old Joseon
(Three Kingdoms Period)

Goguryeo
B.C.37-A.D.668
Subak,deokgyeoni

Baekje
B.C.18 - A.D.661
Subak,subakhui,subyeokta

Silla
B.C.57 - A.D.676
Gukseondo, subak, subyeok, taekgyeon, etc.

Unified Silla
676 - 935

Goryeo
918 - 1392

Joseon
1392 - 1910

Japanese Colonial Period
1910 - 1945
(A crisis facing a threat of exterminating traditional Korean martial arts)
Karate, taegyeon, dangsu

Repubic of Korea
August 15, 1945 to the present
Dangsudo, taesudo, taekwondo, subakdo, and so on
(all unified into taekwondo on August 5, 1965)

In the meantime, King Jeongjo of Joseon in 1790 A.D. ordered Lee Deok-mu and Pak Je-ga to compile a martial arts book, entitled *The Muyedobo-tongji* (an illustrated martial arts book). Vol. IV of the book under the title of *gwonbeop* (the fist arts) carried detailed drawings of various martial arts movements and forms. A few scholars contend that the book of *gwonbeop* was an imitation of a Chinese martial arts book *Gihyo-sinseo* written by Je Guiguang in the days of Ming dynasty in China; however, Hwang Gi, the founder of Mudeokgwan Taekwondo School after national liberation from Japanese colonial rule, claims in his *Subakdo Textbook* that it is authentic to say that the Ming dynasty of China rather introduced the *subak* martial arts from Korea because *subak* was already very popular earlier in the days of Goguryeo (part of Korea).

Available documents and monuments for historical verification

Old Joseon : *Handan-gogi, Gyuwon-sahwa* (historical tales)

Three Kingdoms : *Haesang-japnok, Haedong-ungi, Samguk-sagi, Jewang-ungi, Joseon Sanggosa* (all historical records), and Goguryeo mural paintings at ancient royal tombs

Unified Silla : Geumgang warriors statues at Seokguram and other Geumgang warriors copper statues

Goryeo : *Goryeosa* (history of Goryeo)

Joseon : *Sejong Sillok, Joseon Wangjo Sillok, Haedong Jukji, Taejong Sillok, Sejo Sillok, Yongjae Chonghwa* (all historical records), *Muyedobo-tongji, Jaemulbo, Daejon Tongpyeon, Byeongjon* (martial arts books), *Sinjung Tonggukyeoji-Seungram* (a geographical guidebook), and others

The Emergence of Contemporary Taekwondo : 1945 up to Present

The liberation of the country from Japanese colonial rule on August 15, 1945 gave birth to a national movement to revive the self-consciousness of the Korean people about their culture and tradition. Long-inherited folk games began to revive and there appeared some people who had been secretly practicing the suppressed martial arts of *taekgyeon*. Among others, a group of martial arts practitioners who gathered around Song Deok-ki (1893-1987) started their vigorous activities, and multiple dojangs (gymnasiums) spread rapidly as Korean students studying in Japan and Korean nationals in China were returning home.

However, for almost 20 years after the national liberation, martial arts taekwondo had to suffer a great hardship due to the rivalry among various taekwondo schools in the midst of turmoil with their repeated separating and regrouping among themselves. Some notable taekwondo schools in the initial stage were Cheongdo-gwan (headed by Lee Won-kuk), Joseon Yonmu-gwan (Chun Sang-sop), Mudeok-gwan (Hwang Gi), YMCA Kwonbop-dojang (Yoon Byong-in), Gaesong Songmu-gwan (Ro Byong-jik), and others. These taekwondo schools tried hard to maintain their dojangs even under the adverse situation of the 1950-1953 Korean War, during the period of which the representatives of various schools, namely, Ro Byong-jik, Yoon Kwae-byeong, Hwang Gi, Lee Jong-wu, Hyeon Jong-myeong, Jo Yeong-ju, and Kim In-hwa, held a meeting in the provisional capital, Busan, to agree for the first time to organize an association called the Daehan Gongsudo Association. A month later, Hwang Gi pulled himself out of the Association and founded an independent Dangsudo Association when the capital returned to Seoul. In the same way, the Korea Taekwondo Association centered around Cheongdo-gwan was founded separately with a view to campaigning for unification of taekwondo groups although it soon had to face its dissolution due to the failure of the campaign.

The Founding of Daehan Taesudo Association

The military coup detat of May 16, 1961, motivated the integration of various martial arts schools under the name of Taesudo. The Ministry of Education under the military government in 1961 adopted a policy to bring all assimilated organizations to a unity, according to which the representatives of independent schools, such as Daehan Subakdo Association, Gongsudo Changmu-gwan, Gongsudo Songmu-gwan, Gangdokwon Mudo Association, and some others, met together to agree on founding the Daehan Taesudo Association on September 16, 1961, as a result of painstaking efforts mainly by Lee Jong-wu, Uhm Un-gyu, Lee Nam-seok, and others.

Chae Myeong-sin became the first president of the Association and the Daehan Taesudo Association was registered at the Korea Amateur Sports Association as an official member sports organization on February 23, 1962. Taesudo debuted on October 4, 1962, as a demonstration sport of the 43rd National Athletic Meet held in Daegu, later becoming an official event of the National Athletic Meet since October 24,1962 (the 44th meet). At that time, there were individual competitions of 7 weight divisions, ranging from fly to heavy, and games were classified into two categories, i.e., Medium-Skill category (1st and 2nd Dan) and High-Skill category (3rd Dan and over).

The First National Fresh Players Championships were held on April 18, 1965, which was followed by the First Presidential Flag-winning National Taesudo Team Tournament held on October 28, 1966.

Subsequently, there followed the 1st Foreign-Residents-in-Korea Individual Championships (June 16, 1968), and the 1st National Primary School Taesudo Championships as well as the first-ever Womens Individual Championships (October 24, 1970). Beginning in 1974, the Collegiate Taesudo Federation organized its independent championships instead of its sectional participation in the national championships held by the Korea Taesudo Association since 1963, thus getting license for its independent participation in the National Athletic Meet, too.

The Appellation of Taekwondo and CI

In the mid-1952, a group of martial arts experts staged a martial arts demonstration before the then President Seung-man Rhee in celebration of his birthday. After a 30-minute demonstration, President Rhee asked the military personnel who participated in the demonstration about the name of the martial arts. Then he was quite vexed at the answering that it was dangsudo coming from China, and immediately retorted, Why is it dangsudo?, commenting that our country has had *taekgyeon* since a long time ago. Later, the military martial arts experts who organized the above demonstration debated on a proper naming of the traditional national martial arts, finally arriving at a conclusion that taekwondo may be an adequate appellation because it involves two meanings of both *taekgyeon* (foot skill) and *subak* (hand skill) for a bare-handed martial arts using the foot and the hand together. Many gave their consent to this idea and the Appellation Committee of the KTA adopted this appellation of taekwondo on April 11, 1955, although the official use of this appellation was put into effect on August 5, 1965.

In the end, taekwondo was designated as a national martial arts when President Park Chung Hee personally presented to the KTA on March 20, 1971, his handwriting with a brush, depicting National Martial Arts Taekwondo.

The government of the Republic of Korea on December 15, 1996, adopted 10 items of symbols for its Corporate Identity (CI) program to represent the typical Korean culture, in which taekwondo was included together with hanbok, Hangeul, gimchi and bulgogi, Bulguksa (temple), Seokguram, Goryeo insam (ginseng), talchum (mask dance), Jongmyo jereak (Royal Shrine ceremonial music), Mt. Seorak, and world-famous

Korean artists. All these items are the most typical of Korea and, at the same time, the most conspicuous by their specialty in the world, thereby deserving to play the main role in globalizing the Korean cultural heritage.

Internationalization of Taekwondo

In 1968, the Korea Amateur Sports Association (KASA) played a go-between in the settlement of the disputes prevailing among various groups of Taekwondo circle. However, disputes prolonged as the heads of 17 gwans (taekwondo schools or gymnasiums) were against the KASAs plan of integration and there still were clashes of opinions between the Korea Taekwondo Association and the International Taekwondo Federation regarding the issue of unifying taekwondo forms (pumsaes) as well as the authority to dispatch taekwondo instructors abroad. In May 1973, the Ministry of Education stepped into taking a drastic measure to nullify the license of the ITF, calming down all controversies. There had existed more than 40 gwans before they were regrouped into 10 main gwans in 1973. It was only in 1978 that the KTA managed to have a complete control of the taekwondo circle by closing down the General Central Gwan of Taekwondo on August 5 and 10 central gwans on October 5 of the year.

A turning point was marked when Dr. Kim Un-yong took office as the 7th president of the KTA in January 1971. Soon after his inauguration, Dr. Kim had Gukgiwon (World Taekwondo Headquarters) built, and organized the next year the 1st World Taekwondo Championships at Gukgiwon, when the delegates from 17 countries joined together to found the World Taekwondo Federation (WTF). The WTF was affiliated in October 1975 to the General Association of International Sports Federations (GAISF) to make taekwondo officially recognized as an international sport. In 1976 taekwondo was adopted as one of the official events by the CISM (International Military Sports Council).

The Promoting Committee for Adoption of Taekwondo as an Olympic Event

The WTF in the early 1994 launched into full-scale preparations for making taekwondo an official Olympic program. A committee was set up for promoting taekwondo as an Olympic event and the WTF launched a massive advertisement campaign, beginning with the organization of the Seoul International Taekwondo Tournament in celebration of the centennial anniversary of the IOC in the hope of displaying a strong will of taekwondo people who aspire to becoming members of the Olympic family.

The Promoting Committee first convened on January 15, 1994, at the Renaissance Hotel in Seoul with the participation of 52 members, Korean and foreign personalities. The committee elected Kim Jip (former sports minister) the president of the committee, Josiah Henson (WTF vice president) the vice president, and Lee Geum-hong (WTF secretary general) the working group secretary, and agreed to set up 4 subcommittees. Kim Jip, president of the Committee, especially emphasized that A pan-national support is required in order to make our traditional martial art sport taekwondo adopted as an official event of the Olympic Games.

The Promoting Committee drew up a plan, as the 1st stage business program, to invite the members of the IOC Commission for the Programme to the Seoul International Taekwondo Tournament in the hope of lobbying them into adoption of an item of agenda regarding the inclusion of taekwondo in the Olympic program at the IOC Commission for the Programme meeting expected in May 1994. For its 2nd and 3rd stage programs, the Committee planned to send out the committee members who were well experienced in sports diplomacy to the countries, where the members of the IOC Commission for the Programme as well as the members of IOC Executive Board with the negative thinking on the matter were staying, to persuade them into a favorable thinking. And, in the final stage, the Committee was to launch a massive PR activities by sending a bidding delegation during the 103rd IOC General Meeting to be held in September in Paris. Especially, Paris, the site of the IOC meeting, was the bastion of karate, a strong rival of taekwondo, and its World Headquarters was seated there. In addition to that, an independent International Taekwondo Federation (ITF) was persistently maneuvering to interrupt the Promotion Committees efforts. Therefore, the Committee had to take precautions against any disagreeable happenings.

Adoption of Taekwondo Event for 2000 Sydney Olympic Games

September 4, 1994, was the day marking a historical event of the national martial art taekwondo for its inclusion in the Olympics at the Paris IOC General Meeting. This success was duly attributable to the elaborate stratagem of the Korean delegation led by IOC Vice President Kim Un-yong (WTF president), which ranged from a blitz presentation of the issue on the agenda to the creation of atmosphere for a favorable voting. The Korean delegation originally had it in mind that the item of agenda on taekwondo would be presented to the IOC General Meeting through the Executive Board which was in session until August 28; however, faced with a strong resistance staged by North Korea (ITF) and Japan (karate), the Korean delegation on second thoughts turned to a complete change of the overall plan to put the agenda item all of a sudden at the last session of the IOC General Meeting.

All such painstaking efforts by the delegation as mentioned above have resulted in making taekwondo an official event for the 2000 Sydney Olympic Games at the Paris IOC General Meeting held on September 4, 1994. With this, taekwondo competitions was staged in Sydney 2000 Olympics with 4 weight divisions for Men's and Women's category, respectively, totaling 8 gold medals in all, which is sure to contribute to the enhancement of international status of Korea as well as to the worldwide dissemination of Korean sports culture.

Chaper **3** *Three*

The Philosopy and Spirit of Taekwondo

3

The Philosophy and Spirit of Taekwondo

The Han Philosophy

Taekwondo is a compound consisting of two words, *taekwon* and *do*. *Taekwon* refers to yin and *do* to yang. *Taekwon* involves a dynamic character and *do* a static one, and the former implicates a physical conception while *do* a metaphysical one. Thus, taekwondo stands on the principles of yin and yang and the *do* constitutes the essence of martial arts. In effect, *do* commands the entire Oriental philosophy as a metaphysical central idea and is usually expressed by the terminology of *taegeuk*. Here, *taegeuk* signifies a unique (*tae*) and supreme (*geuk*) metaphysical truth governing the natural state of the cosmos. Oriental philosophers say that *taegeuk* is the essential creator of the existence and value of all things in the universe before heaven (yang) and earth (yin) were divided, and the state of *taegeuk* produced yin and yang, from which the five elements of the universe were originated. Therefore, the Korean people adopted *taegeuk* as the symbol of the Korean race, adapting themselves to the principles of yin-yang variation.

The Independence Arch in Seoul caries a carving of the prototype of *taegeuk* flag, a national symbol of Korea. The flag has at the center an emblem of *taegeuk* and 4 different symbols of *gwe*, each at the corner of the flag. You will eventually come across with the patterns of those *gwes* (in 8 detailed forms) and *taegeuk* in the course of practicing taekwondo because the training units of Pumsaes Taegeuk and Palgwe, each ranging from Jang 1 to Jang 8, derive from the principles of *taegeuk*.

The emblem of *taegeuk* is usually drawn to express two duplicated circles in the form of cycling according to the yin-yang theory of *Juyeok* (The Book of Changes); however, the ancient form of the *taegeuk* emblem as recorded in the old records of *Handan-gogi* carries triple circles representing heaven, earth, and human being, which is the original form of *taegeuk* for the Korean race. This *taegeuk* emblem was described after the shape of two folding hands (the left hand clasping the right hand), which was called *gongsu*. By doing *gongsu*, one thinks of the heaven with one's mind in concentration, which is the veritable meaning of the *taegeuk* emblem. Today, the ancient form of *taegeuk* emblem is still used largely in the field of arts and crafts in that the craftsmen want to express their aspiration for something to link with the abstruse mystery of the universe.

The theory of *taegeuk* derives from the thought of Triple Essence in Unity, which is the ideal of *Hongik-ingan* (humanitarianism); therefore, *taegeuk* is an emblem of the *Hongik-ingan* ideal. The emblem of *taegeuk* shows an image of the combination of three curved beads, as if containing three smaller circles (heaven, earth, and human being) inside a larger circle. The three elements, i.e., heaven, earth, and human being, are depicted in the shapes of a circle (○/•), a square (□/—), and an angle (△/I). The triple essence consisting of heaven, earth, and human being is sometimes called *samjae*, which means *samgeuk* (triple essence) is one entity or one contains three or three gather together to return to a unity.

The expression of *han* in the old records of *Handan-gogi* signifies that all are collected to make one. Also, *hana* (one) is the core ideal of *Hongik-ingan*, which is the ideology of national founding by Dangun, the progenitor of the Korean race, who advocated the thought of peace by teaching that human beings must be made great and beneficial to people at large.

Han is indeed the proper idea of the Korean people. It is the spiritual root for the Korean people, having various meanings, such as great, high, light, bright, and one as a whole like yin-yang making one. In short, *han* is the central idea of the *Han* philosophy, which implies that in a human being mind and body are not separable from each other, nor separable are heaven and human being because they are destined to be in unity and in harmony. In the theory of existence, the idea of *Han* could be regarded as the original creation along with all things in the universe.

The practice of taekwondo eyes mastering both the physical and mental aspects of the *Han* philosophy. The principles and ideas of the *Han* philosophy are applied to the principle of taekwondo: the symbols of circle, square, and triangle, which represent the triple essence, i.e., heaven, earth, and human being, delineate the basics of all movements in taekwondo. A circle mark meaning a revolution represents the energy to make one move, a square mark meaning a stance represents the base, and a triangle mark meaning the form of arms represents the technique, thus all the three combined into one (*han*) making a complete movement.

The movements of taekwondo involve such effective techniques as may be adopted from the shape and posture, and contact and interaction of things in the universe, especially imitating many natural images which most likely reflect the nature of consistency between the human being and the universe. Therefore, the system of taekwondo techniques has something to do with cosmology and homology which are discussed in the theory of the universe. In taekwondo, the mark • (point) implies the principle of revolution made by a technique and power in all forms of defense (yin) and offense (yang) actions; the mark — implies a stability of the base; and the mark | represents the center line to keep balance of the body like the spine. Thus, all taekwondo movements can be explained as a process of varying in actions of those three forms, i.e., •, —, and |. This is the core of the theory of the body in the *Han* philosophy.

Taekwondo as martial arts involves experiencing concrete movements of the body, each movement focusing on the maintenance of a unity between mind and body. This principle of unity comes from the idea that the whole is one, i.e., *han*. Therefore, the system of taekwondo techniques originates from the principle of *han* characterized by *samjae*, the triple essence (heaven, earth, and human being). Peoples daily life of practicing taekwondo is aimed at accomplishing this *han*, as a principle of the cosmic system as well as a philosophical principle.

In conclusion, the *Han* philosophy in taekwondo pursues an ideal that the little universe, human being, as the subject of *han*, links up with the large universe, nature, to become one entity. Therefore, a series of taekwondo training, beginning with Pumsae Taegeuk (the large universe) and ending with Pumsae Ilyeo (the symbols of all kinds of goodness in human life), must be connected with a thinking in the dimension of the universe.

A Series of Taekwondo Pumsaes

Pumsae	Pumsae Line	No. of Pums	No. of Movements Level of Skills
Taegeuk 1 jang	18	20	Gewp grades and 1st Dan or Pum grades
Taegeuk 2 jang	18	23	
Taegeuk 3 jang	20	34	
Taegeuk 4 jang	20	29	
Taegeuk 5 jang	20	32	
Taegeuk 6 jang	19	31	
Taegeuk 7 jang	25	33	
Taegeuk 8 jang	27	38	
Goryeo	30	45	2nd Dan or Poom
Geumgang	27	35	3rd Dan or Poom
Taebaek	26	38	4th Dan or Poom
Pyeongwon	21	25	5th Dan
Sipjin	28	31	5th and 6th Dan
Jitae	28	37	6th and 7th Dan
Cheongwon	26	27	7th Dan
Hansu	27	34	8th Dan
Ilyeo	23	27	9th Dan

- A grade of skill, Poom, which equals Dan, is given only to the trainees under age 15, who may obtain their grades up to 4th Pum; however, their Pum is changed to Dan when they become over 15 years old.

The Spirit of Taekwondo

The spirit of taekwondo is referred to the value of the most desired human personality which one hopes to attain through the practice of taekwondo. One can achieve the spirit of taekwondo by experiencing and perceiving the truth of taekwondo techniques in the course of training. The following points must be taken into consideration for attaining this objective:

1. *Cheonin-habil* (Heaven and Human Being in Oneness)

The Korean philosophy, inclusive of legendary tales of the Korean national founder Dangun, in principle, seeks the thought of peace which can be attained through the maintenance of balance and harmony in the course of the endless recurrence of creations and variations among the tripartite essentials of the universe (*samjae*), i.e., heaven, earth, and human being.

The philosophy of Yulgok and Toegye, grand masters of metaphysics, explains all the creation — whether it is nature of the universe or human beings or things — with the concept of principles and atmospheric force. According to this theory, *taegeuk* gives birth to yin and yang, which develop into Four Elements and Eight Gaes, dominating the life of human beings with such symmetrical concepts as the principles and the atmospheric force, heaven and earth, day and night, left and right, dynamic and static, slow and fast, curve and straight, and the like.

The concepts of *taegeuk* philosophy, which can be expounded by the principles and the atmospheric force, are also applicable to the little universe of human beings. As one may distinguish the body from mind in reckoning the existence of a human being, so is it possible to differentiate the theories of philosophy between the Orient and the Occident (between body-mind dualism and monism) depending on how the relationship of the two is to be thought. Yulgok analogized the principles and the atmospheric force with the metaphysical *do* and the physical *gi* (vessel) in explaining the phenomena of all the existence. *Do* is related to the metaphysical principles while *gi* is the physical material or vessel with which the principles can be embodied. On the other hand, Toegye maintained a dualistic concept regarding the principles (*ri*) and the atmospheric force (*gi*), interpreting the principles (*ri*) as the invisible metaphysical means to justify the reason for existence of certain things. Therefore, the *ri* (principles) can also be identified with *taegeuk* or *do*.

If we try to analyze the movements of taekwondo techniques from the concept of *ri* and *gi*, the cause of a movement is the mechanism of *ri* and the result of a movement is brought about by the operation of *gi*. At the time of conducting gyeorugi or pumsae, it is the best way to apply the principles of *ri* and *gi* in making one movement after another. The movement of an exquisite technique can be achieved only through incessant hard training in a way of applying the *ri-gi* principles, such as the simultaneity and momentary swiftness of thought (*ri*) and action (*gi*) or the harmony of mind and body. The attainment of the highest level of exquisite techniques is referred to the reach to the state of *cheonin-hapil* as expressed by the Yulgok philosophy, and the state of *dalin* (master-hand) or *ipsin* (master of divinity) as usually expressed in the taekwondo circle.

In this way, the philosophical thoughts of the Korean race have become the central ideas to formulate the spirit of taekwondo, serving as the fundamental criteria governing the philosophical and kinetic principles of taekwondo art. The training of taekwondo itself means one is determined not only to attain the highest skill of taekwondo techniques but ultimately try to reach the state of *simsin-ilyeo* (mind-body in unity), *cheonin-hapil* (heaven-earth in oneness), and then to become a *hongik-ingan* (humanitarian one). The training of taekwondo itself is ones philosophical bodily actions and the daily activities of taekwondo practitioners are a philosophical life.

2. *Hongik-ingan* (Humanitarianism)

Unlike many other sports, the practice of taekwondo sport weighs the spiritual aspect the most, and its final object is to cultivate a person with a strong moral conscience. The virtue of taekwondo training, which aims at perfection of an all-around human being, can be well manifested in ones achievement of the mind of *hongik-ingan* through the enhancement of harmony between mind and body, thereby believing in the merits of living in homologous cooperation between human beings and other human beings or between human beings and nature. Therefore, taekwondo training must be conducted in a close coordination among the spiritual, moral, and physical training, which are inseparable from one another. The thoughts of *Han* philosophy adopted by taekwondo particularly focus on natures qualities, with which all things grow and prosper in the relationships of coexistence and homology. These thoughts are exactly represented by the thought of *hongik-ingan,* the ideology of national founding invented by the Korean progenitor, Dangun, which emphasizes making the human world broadly beneficial.

The terminology of *hongik-ingan* appears in the historical records describing the founding of Old Joseon in the *Samguk-yusa* (Histories of the Three Kingdoms) and also in the *Jewang-ungi* (Royal History) and the *Gyuwon-sahwa* (Historical Tales). Human beings grow and live surrounded by the heaven, earth, and nature, thus keeping in themselves all qualities of the three.

In training taekwondo, the targets of both attack and blocking are classified into three parts of the human body, i.e., *arae* (the lower part), *momtong* (trunk), and *eolgul* (face), corresponding with the triple essence of the universe, heaven, earth and nature. Especially, the earth which accommodates all the creation is believed to breathe to live like all living creatures, giving out the feeling of a unity with human beings.

The earth breathes to make air circulate. Also, breathing is essential for the human being to sustain life. Therefore, taekwondo considers the breathing as an important element to be trained because an adequate way of breathing helps sharpen the corporal senses and enhance corporal functions in the course of making movements.

Through practicing taekwondo, one can polish one's mind and body just like air always circulates. The process of taekwondo training is equal to the process of seeking a harmonious development and balance of both mind and body.

Taekwondo also adopts the quality of nature in refining trainee's spirit. The virtues of benevolence, which is an innate character of the human being, are the same as the qualities of nature. Virtue means an act done exactly as the mind instructs. Therefore, the virtue of benevolence should be the essence of philosophy inherent in the spirit of taekwondo.

In conclusion, we see that the spirit of taekwondo comes from the thought of *hongik-ingan*, which looks to cultivate virtues of benevolence. *Hongik-ingan* is the consciousness of harmony and order inherent in human life, and it is the philosophy of life which respects lives of all living things. The cultivation of such spirit of benevolence can be achieved through taekwondo training, which is a philosophical act out of the conscience of morality innate in oneself.

3. *Simsin-ilyeo* (Mind-body in Oneness)

Mind and body or flesh and spirit is the expression referring to the essential concept related to human existence. A German word Person meaning the body has also other derivative meanings, such as a person, one's self, and an individual, alluding a human life in general. On the other hand, mind signifies all that is related to the spiritual functions, such as one's consciousness, sentiments and ideas; or, it refers to the whole thing related to one's spiritual functions, in addition to one's inborn character or quality, and one's opinions, sentiments and feelings which are not visible and vary depending on circumstances.

Philosopher Toegye used such words as heart, sentiment, will, and justice in expressing the concept of mind, and defined that mind is the governor of the flesh, while Philosopher Yulgok regarded mind as meaning nature, sentiment, and justice. The relationship between mind and body may be expressed in such terms as yin-yang, static-dynamic, *ri-gi* (principle-atmospheric force), time-space, existence-nonexistence, technical skill-thinking, and others. Also, mind or spirit is a metaphysical term as a superior concept while body a physical term as an inferior concept.

The practice of taekwondo can be regarded as the process of practical training to make trainees enhance their personalities or become veritable human beings through repeated refinements of their mind and body. In our daily life, it is difficult to clearly distinguish the word body from flesh. However, the body is generally used to mean a human body and the flesh infers something of a material concept regarding the human body.

The relationship between mind and body customarily viewed in our daily life can be summarized into three categories as follows:

First, mind gives influence on the body (spiritualists).

Second, to the contrary, the body influences mind (materialists).

Third, mind and the body are equally balanced with each other (monists).

However, people ordinarily view the body as an exterior world and mind as an interior world. One can convey what one's mind experiences, i.e., one's ideas, only through one's physical actions, e.g., bodily movements (kicking, punching, etc.), speaking, writing, and others.

In taekwondo training, the body is trained for physical fitness and mind for the refinement of spirit.

Since taekwondo is characterized by the techniques of deadly blows even with a single stroke of either hand or foot, the training of techniques must be simultaneously accompanied by the spiritual training, which is aimed at character building by means of arming the trainees with the senses of modesty, justice, and keeping order, as well as the power of inner control with the spirit of outer tenderness and inner rigidity. The body is governed by the power of mind, and the power of mind comes from the association of physical exercises and the senses.

Mind has no forms, and the aspects of all forms vary under the control of mind. This means formless mind is reflected on the outer world in various forms. In doing pumsae or gyeorugi in taekwondo, the aspect or form of a movement, which is called *pum* in taekwondo, is a manifestation of the body (a function of *gi*), and what commands that movement is mind (a function of *ri*). The taekwondo training is a bodily activity and at the same time a spiritual or mind training.

Taekwondo eyes attaining oneness of mind and body — *simsin-ilyeo* or *simsin-hapil* — in order to make one arrive at the highest level of idealistic human character. Various faculties of both mind and body should not be regarded as separable between mind and body and they should rather be considered each as part of the whole. The training and enhancement of any of those faculties, whatever course it may take, must be always directed to one common center, that is, character building.

Thus, all different ways in which various faculties of mind and body are developed are to converge on one point leading to a single way (*do*) for perfection of character building.

Do (Moral Doctrine)

Beginning with taekwondo, many Oriental martial arts like judo, geomdo (fencing), and hapgido (art of self-defense) have all a suffix *do* in their names, which denotes martial arts. The term *do* is the principal thought of Taoism represented by Lao-tze and Chung-tze and widely used by Buddhists and Confucians, too.

The word *do* first appeared in Lao-tzes Morality Classics, in which he explained *do* is the source and origin of the universe. *Do* is, so to speak, a formless body being an absolute spiritual substance beyond time and space. Lao-tze also said, in the Hanfeitze, that *Do* is the origins of all things in the universe and the mystical guideline of all principles. The origin of the term *do* can be analyzed in two ways, one from the viewpoint of the pictographic symbols of a Chinese character and the other from Korean phonemes. The Chinese character *do* is a compound of the symbol meaning a man's body in the form of walking swinging the arms back and forth and another meaning the head, thus inferring that one thinks while walking. Therefore, *do* comprises practical philosophy in that it involves both thinking and acting.

In the Korean language, *do* derives from the etymology of *dopneunda* (to help). The Confucian writings, Four Books-Five Classics, all contain the system of *do* philosophy, writing about helping and being helped. We can find in many places of Confucian Classics the expressions regarding *do*: for example, harming and killing is *bido* (against *do*) and when *do* is exercised, there is *cheonha-yudo* (there is *do* in the world) and *cheonha-mudo* (no *do* in the world) in case of ignoring *do*. If *do* mean's to help, it is exactly the humanitarian *do* which is the core of Dangun's ideology termed as the thought of *hongik-ingan*. The spirit of *hongik-ingan* orders one to lead a veritably humane life by means of helping others broad and wide.

In the Oriental thoughts, a human being is viewed as an integral whole and not separable in two identities of spirit and body. Likewise, taekwondo also teaches that spirit and the body are a one unit to be trained simultaneously. Taekwondo as martial arts basically stands on the thought of *simsin-ilyo* (mind-body in oneness). In other words, the ultimate goal of taekwondo training is to make one resolve by oneself how to refine ones body and mind by trying to achieve the state of *simsin-ilyo* voluntarily and actively on the basis of the human instinct to live in harmony with nature.

In taekwondo, a combination of *taekwon* and *do* should be extended till its perfection. If *taekwon* is the human body, then *do* is spirit or mind; and, if the former is dynamic, the latter is static. Furthermore, *taekwon* represents an act of comprehensive practice which is visible, while *do* does one's intuition directing that act invisibly. Therefore, the practice of taekwondo requires the development of internal intuition (mind) as well as external practice (body). Taekwondo through its training must finally lead to a perfection of human character following the work of elevating various balanced functions of mind and body from the normal standard to beyond the normal one.

The philosophical aspect of *do* in taekwondo can be exposed by one's intuition of action, which can be refined through experiences of mind and body in the course of training the system of foot-hand techniques, gyeorugi, and others. Taekwondo, which is martial arts in nature, aims at achieving oneness of body and mind along with the enhancement of self-recognition resulting from the strengthening of spiritual concentration power, always harmonizing oneself with nature. The practice of taekwondo is also an education of the whole man and an education for self-consciousness of one's own experiences, which is characterized by the training of all parts of the body in natural sequence in the fashion of the Oriental training.

The key point to be emphasized in Oriental sports like taekwondo is doing personal experiences in the form of self-training. One may arrive at a comprehension of the *Han* philosophy in taekwondo when one can involve oneself in intuition, thereby enjoying one's life and deeply looking into the inside of ones being even during the process of practicing, without merely seeking any physical fitness or technical skill to win a game.

Ye (Courtesy)

Ye is an order of the universe. With this order all things in the universe can be distinguished from one another. *Ye* means primarily the rules and principles which sustain the order of nature before it is understood to be a formal etiquette or courtesy. There are the principles to keep the order of heaven and earth in the universe, while human society has its own principles to keep its order. The spirit of *ye* can be well manifested in the spirit of modesty which makes one behave humble in human relations with others. Therefore, the essence of *ye* lies in discrimination and it can be regarded as a certain formula of social contract, functioning as an agent to keep the senses of values maintained in society.

In the *Book of Rites*, Confucius said, *Ye* means controlling all things to make them put in order. Thus, *ye* takes its root in the traditional Confucian views. Confucianism uses the term *ye* as an expression of being human, regarding it as the norm of the most basic and civilized behaviors that must be conducted by human beings. In Confucianism, *ye* denotes various meanings, such as benevolence, righteousness, respect, loyalty and trust, all related to Confucian virtues.

Especially in taekwondo, one makes it a rule to focus on modesty, harmony, and order as a practical observance of *ye*. In all forms of martial arts including taekwondo, their practitioners evaluate *ye* highly by saying, begin with *ye* and end in *ye*. At each time of beginning and ending the taekwondo training, the trainees make a bow of salutation under the command of *gyeongrye*, which implies *ye*. This makes trainees keep themselves in neat appearances and attitudes all the time and pay respect to others from the bottom of heart. Taekwondo practitioners at the time of training especially pay much attention to their attire, trying to wear *doboks* (uniforms) and girdles neatly, which is an act of observing *ye*. Observing *ye* is an act of respecting the other party, helping after all keep one's own prestige.

It has been a longtime tradition that a strict courtesy and discipline between seniors and juniors as well as invisible norms of order is maintained among taekwondo practitioners. This kind of ethical virtues are the first things to be trained in the initial stage of practicing Oriental martial arts. In May 1971, the Korea Taekwondo Association established a code of etiquette for taekwondo practitioners to observe not only at the *dojang* but in their daily life. It is a general rule for taekwondoists to express their etiquette (*ye*) in a standing position. First, one's expression of courtesy must be necessarily accompanied by an attitude of respect and confidence regardless of the other party's position, higher or lower.

Second, one's appearance must be always neat and graceful at the time of expressing one's courtesy.

Third, one should express courtesy by bowing the upper body by 15 degrees.

Taekwondo practitioners bow whenever they enter or leave their *dojang,* where they acquire techniques and, at the same time, refine their body and mind to achieve *do,* that is to say, making themselves perfect human beings. It is especially important that trainees must show their respect, loyalty, and trust toward their masters, not to mention about the mutual expression of respect and confidence among fellow trainees. Even during any official competitions or training of matches, one should always regard ones opponent as an excellent training partner.

Dobok (Uniform)

Dobok, the martial arts uniform for taekwondo, consists of three parts, i.e., pants, jacket, and girdle (*tti*), which signify *samgeuk* (triple essence) and are called a *han* assembly all together, meaning a philosophical *han.* The *dobok* much resembles the traditional Korean costume, *hanbok* whose inventor has not been traced as yet.

There are many records about the *hanbok* pants in the classics of *Samguk-sagi, Silla Dynasty, Samguk-yusa,* and *Garak-gukgi,* and even Chinese books of history carried records of Korean pants worn by the people of Goguryeo, Baekje, and Silla on the Korean peninsula. At the time of Song in China, Xukei wrote the *Goryeo-dogyeong,* an illustrative book concerning Goryeo, in which he mentioned that *jouiseonins* in Goguryeo wear a white-color ramie clothing with a black-color silk girdle around the waist. The word *joui* of *jouiseonin* means one has a black girdle on oneself, from which, it seems, today's custom of wearing black belts among martial artists was derived. The long-hanging jacket and pants in white color worn by *jouiseonins*, martial artists in Goguryeo, are vividly shown on the mural paintings of warriors found at the tombs of the Three-Kingdom's era.

The *dobok* of taekwondo, resembling the *hanbok* in its design of cutting, shows three patterns of circle, square, and triangle in both pants and jacket, respectively. For example, the waist part of pants makes a round form, the cloth attached to the waist line is in the shape of a square, and the further attachment of pants makes the form of a triangle. The same way goes with the jacket, too. Unlike the fashions of other clothes, the pattern of *dobok* has rarely changed because of its conservatism. It is most likely that *jouiseonins* of Goguryeo inherited the white-color costume from a similar one used by *gukjarang* (elite students) in the Old Joseon era.

The tradition of martial arts which prevailed in the days of Old Joseon must have been passed down to *jouiseonins* of Goguryeo and *hwarangs* of Silla in the Three-Kingdoms era. And, the above-mentioned circle, square, and triangle represent heaven, earth, and human being, respectively, which are the triple essence making *han* (oneness). The *hanbok*, the origin of *dobok*, takes its pattern of positioning the jacket and pants after the principle explained in a philosophical book, *Chonbugyeong*, which applies a numerical concept, counting heaven one the first, earth one the second, and human being one the third. Also, according to the principle of yin-yang in the *Book of Changes*, the pants of *dobok* corresponds to yin or earth, the jacket to yang or heaven, and the girdle a human being, which exactly matches the theory of *samgeuk* or *samjae* (heaven, earth, and human being). This thought of *samjae* can be perceived in the structure of almost all the traditional necessities of life, including the Korean topcoat, lady's cloak, and others, apart from the *hanbok* skirt, jacket, and pants, which proves how deeply the Korean people have been influenced by the thought.

However, in July 1978, the taekwondo *dobok* was officially classified into three models with a slight variation in their patterns: an original one for Geup-grade holders; a *dobok* for Pum holders (childrens black belts) having the collar of jacket with two stripes of different colors, red and black; and a *dobok* for Dan holders (black belts) with the collar of jacket in all black color, resembling the shape of an inverted triangle.

The white color for the ground of *dobok* comes from the philosophical thought of the Korean race characterized by the *Han* philosophy, which sees the universe is in white color and the origins of all things also in white color. This phoneme *han*, a derivative of *han* (one), comes from the word *huida* (to be white), which originally means the essence of the universe. A special importance is attached to the taekwondo *dobok* due to its philosophical significance encouraging the polishing of mind and body in a clean *do* uniform.

Tti (Girdle)

The *tti*, a girdle or belt used in taekwondo, is a component of a set of *dobok* together with pants and jacket. Just as the *dobok* is classified into three models for Geup-holders, Pum holders and Dan black belts, so the *tti* has three different types, one for Geup-grade, another for Pum, and a third for Dan black belts. In both cases, the principle of *samgeuk* is applied.

It was customary for the Korean race to believe that among the 3 elements of *samjae* (or *samgeuk)* two elements of heaven and earth were incorporated into a third element, human being, that is called the little universe in the *Han* philosophy. Likewise, in taekwondo *dobok*, the jacket and pants are referred to heaven and earth, respectively, and the *tti* represents the universe comprising the former two. While the *dobok* as a whole gives out a static image, the *tti* alone at the center of *dobok* looks in a dynamic air.

The *tti* has 5 different colors: white for beginners; yellow, blue, and red for Geup-grade holders according to their levels of skill; and black for Dan black belts. The original colors of *samgeuk* are represented by yellow, blue, and red, and white and black colors are the symbols of yin-yang, representing sun-moon, day-night, beginning-completion, and the like. The meaning of those 5 colors can be inferred from the philosophy of yin-yang and the five elements of the universe.

In the Oriental philosophy, yin-yang is believed to be the principle of creating the universe and maintaining order of the universe. The five elements of the universe, representing water, fire, wood, metal, and earth, are the principles of creating heaven and earth. Inside the body of a human being, there exist five viscera and six entails. The five viscera consist of kidney (water), heart (fire), liver (wood), lungs (metal), and spleen (earth). There are also five azimuths: the center (center of the world), east, west, north and south.

In this way, the 5 colors of *tti* can be alluded to the five elements of the universe and the five viscera of the body. It is still noteworthy that even today those five colors are the favorites of the Korean people as traditional colors, which are frequently used in dress ornaments, folk drawings, package paper, etc., aside from the painting of modern constructions, such as royal palaces or temples.

In taekwondo, Geup and Dan have 9 grades, respectively, meaning 9 steps from beginning to completion. The figure 9 comes from the numbering of heaven, earth, yin, yang, plus 5 elements of the universe. On the other hand, the color of *tti* varies in the process of practicing taekwondo in accordance with the principle of the five elements of the universe, and it also symbolizes the five viscera, which are considered to be the sources of life in the phenomena of *gi* (atmospheric force) formulated in the course of endless repetitions of breaking up and gathering of cosmic *gi* (force) within one's self.

The dynamic character of *tti* in an ontological explanation can be referred to *che* (substance) and *yong* (employment), and the *Han* philosophy may be applied to explain its changing motions. The *che* of a *tti* is like a square (earth), the *yong* like a circle (heaven), and a triangle (human being) is made out of them. When one girdles a *tti* around himself, it makes a form of circle, and when one makes a knot by tying the girdle, it forms a triangle, the *tti* itself representing a square (earth). Here, the principle of *samjae* (heaven, earth, human being) is also applied to explain the dynamic character of *tti* (girdle).

Delivering two hard strokes in the abdomen (*danjeon*) with the *tti* after putting on a *dobok* is for the purpose to converge *gi* in the abdomen and convert it into techniques because the *danjeon* is the place where yin and yang meet. In reality, taewkondo practitioners assume it very important to strictly observe *ye* (courtesy) in handling and keeping their *dobok* as if they deal with a symbol of the universe. Therefore, a strict order is required in training taekwondo and that order can be maintained by the establishment of authority and a definite relationship between superiors and inferiors among trainees by means of differentiating the colors of *tti*.

A beginner of taekwondo at first has to wear a white-color *dobok*, because the white color symbolizes a state of nil before any creation or beginning, i.e., *taegeuk*. The yellow symbolizes a birth, and the blue represents rebirth, revival, hope, and youth. Then comes the red-color *tti* to be finally followed by the black belt. Therefore, a beginner must undergo a long painstaking training of sweat blood before attaining a black belt, as if practicing a *do*.

In conclusion, the significance of the *tti* (girdle) in taekwondo lies in its origination from the principles of five elements of the universe, five colors, and five viscera (or *gi*), which require a passage of laborious training. In a comprehensive sense, the *tti* itself reflects the nature of martial arts based on the *Han* philosophy.

Dojang (Gymnasium)

A place for practicing taekwondo is now usually called a gymnasium instead of a traditional name, *dojang*. In general, a gymnasium is meant by a place where a study or functional physical training is conducted for health and fitness or for games only. It appears that the name of *dojang* has been gradually transformed into the modern name of gymnasium due to the fade-out of the concept of *do* in traditional martial arts, including taekwondo, in the process of their becoming the events for sports games.

One characteristic of the practice of taekwondo is that various functions of mind and body are not viewed as separate ones but as an integral one to form human personality so that a continuous training of taekwondo may lead to the perfection of a human being, from which the traditional name of *dojang* derives. People call *dojang* for a place where physical bodily training and metaphysical training are conducted simultaneously. Many other martial arts using the suffix *do*, such as geomdo, judo, and hapgido, also have their own traditions of training *do*, thereby using the name of *dojang* for their training sites.

The practice of taekwondo in nature seeks achieving a oneness of mind and body, and in its initial stage tries to turn all techniques into spontaneous bodily actions, that is, automatism of technical movements, through repeated training of the body. In the process of this training the spirit or mind, which manipulates all physical activities acts as a commander. Therefore, it is important for everyone to conceive that the training of techniques alone is not sufficient but that every movement of physical activities must be accompanied by a simultaneous mental exercise because both should be complementary with each other.

Nonetheless, it is generally observed that beginners experience difficulties in moving the body as they want to; for, bodily movements are apt to resist mental instructions, so to speak, objectivity countering against subjectivity. Mind and body exhibit two qualities, subjective and objective, in expressing one's existence. Therefore, taekwondo through practice aims at bringing in accord the minds directives and the bodily movements, which means submitting the body to subjectivity by overcoming the confrontation between the two different qualities. For instance, one performs a pumsae almost unconsciously without making a slight error in making movements or, in gyeorugi, one reacts automatically to the opponents chagi (kick) attack with a counterattack, which can be done only in a state of oneness of mind and body. This means the body moves automatically at a flash of the minds thinking.

When one speaks of taekwondo, he explains that taekwondo is the way of cultivating a human being by enhancing the truthfulness of human beings, or taekwondo is the way of cultivating a human being by means of training the qualities of self-control, self-restraint, and autonomous spirit as well as the spirit to respect justice and courtesy so that one can preserve through all ones life a philosophy of life based on those qualities.

The mental exercise in taekwondo eyes not merely memorizing the bodily movements in the brain as a means of studying but linking toilsome and repetitive bodily movements with the strengthening of spirit, ultimately leading to the self-consciousness of truths in a human life. *Dojang*, a traditional name of the site for practicing martial arts, is the very place where one can practice the philosophies of *simsin-ilyeo* and *cheonin-hapil*, with which to polish ones mind and body and perceive the principles of one in multiplicity and static state in dynamic state.

Chaper **4** *Four*

The Principles of Taekwondo

4

The Principles of Taekwondo

Three Principles of Taekwondo

Taekwondo is a physical exercise using the four members of the body, i.e., the arms and the legs, and is composed of a series of offense and defense techniques mainly for the purpose of self-defense. The physical exercise of taekwondo helps make one's body and mind strong and sound so that it may enrich one's daily life, and the self-defensive functions of its techniques are based on the application of philosophical principles, such as the ethics of *ri-gi* (basic principles and the atmospheric force), and the *Han* principles of *Juyeok* or *Han* philosophy.

A Greek philosopher Platon referred to a person as the little universe, and also the substance of the Oriental philosophies including the *Han* philosophy is basically related to the thought of a human being as the little universe. The old Dongi culture, the root of the Korean culture, already indicated the parallelism of *taegeuk* thought with *samgeuk* thought referring to heaven, earth, and human being. Taekwondo as national martial arts of Korea has maintained a series of techniques, which are based on the *samgeuk* thought as well as the *taegeuk* thought. Therefore, taekwondo's proper philosophy and principles have been formulated out of these two thoughts.

1. The Principle of *Ri-gi* Ethics

A taekwondo technique consists of a chain of alternate defense and offense movements. These movements conform with the thought of *taegeuk* which involves a unity of mind and body, and follow the principles of *ri-gi*, yin-yang, and dynamics/statics. If a blocking is referred to yin and statics, then an attack by chagi (kicking) or jireugi (punching) corresponds to yang and dynamics. And, a separate movement of technique is the outcome of a cause and a result, which corresponds with the origination as a *ri* phenomenon and the manifestation as a *gi* phenomenon.

According to the Oriental theory of *ri-gi*, the spiritual phenomena found in a person are interpreted as *ri*, while the source of energy which brings about those phenomena is interpreted as *gi*. The *ri-gi* theory is also a kind of symbolism. From the viewpoint of taekwondo culture, the *ri* corresponds with makgi (blocking), jireugi, chagi, the selection of a target, and others, which show aspects of a principle, while the *gi* represents the intensity of power, slowness or fastness of a speed, etc., which show phenomenal aspects of a physical manifestation.

According to the theory of *ri-gi*, each person is born with his/her own four innate characters, i.e., benevolence, righteousness, courtesy, and wisdom, which are the *ri* phenomena as the norms of internal values, and, at the same time, with seven emotions, namely, delight, anger, sorrow, fear, love, hatred, and desire, which are the *gi* phenomena revealing his/her disposition. However, all these characters and emotions may differ in their muddiness and purity depending on each individual person.

Through practicing, taekwondo practitioners learn the norms of ethics, such as the sense of self confidence, courage, the wisdom of discrimination, the spirit of justice, and others, says Lee Jong-wu, a grand master of taekwondo. Therefore, taekwondo is the martial arts which helps its practitioners resolve the task of practical ethics regarding how to embody their true character through spiritual training. When one joins a taekwondo dojang (gymnasium), one has to undergo a hard physical training which can be done only by sweating blood with a strong will of self-control and patience. Then, one enters a higher stage of training to learn basic movements, pumsaes, and finally gyeorugi, which are a series of training subjects. During the process of repeating this series of training, the trainees may improve their body and mind and achieve a better coordination between the spirit and the body.

This kind of training which is devised to follow the principles of *ri-gi* ethics ultimately aims at raising a truly humanistic human being. Taekwondo training is, in essence, a conduct of practical philosophy because it eyes polishing one's mind as well as enhancing one's personal character through a systematic training of the body. Man is a spiritual and physical real existence, an existence governed by the *ri-gi* principles. Being a *ri-gi* existence requires the attainment of concord, reconciliation, and harmony.

2. The Principle of *Yeokhak* (the Science of Changes) in *Han* Philosophy

All taekwondo movements and the body in the *yeokhak* theory accommodate the principles of *samgeuk* (heaven, earth, human being) and they are explained by the symbols, i.e., point (•), surface (—), and line (|). *Gi,* which can be referred to a technique in terms of the *gi* principles, means a *yeokhak* energy, varying depending on the high and low of the center of gravity and the long and short of the base. Also, in terms of the *yeokhak* principles of bodily movements, the point (•) represents a revolving and cycling movement, the surface (—) the base as well as the direction toward the target, and the line (|) the center of gravity as the lifeline existent in the body. Noteworthy is that the stability as defined in taekwondo and the static state of a substantive material are not of the same meaning.

Especially in the practice of taekwondo gyeorugi, a competitor has to swiftly respond to his opponents ever-changing diverse movements by immediately changing his own stance, which requires an ability of reaction and adaptable tactics. If the vertical line of the center of gravity moves beyond the limit of the base (stance), one has to swiftly move his foot to restructure a new base, which must be accompanied by the control of acceleration.

Space and time, which consist of the 3 basic elements of physics, i.e., mass, time, and distance, are not absolute but relative among one another depending on the speed of an object according to the theory of relativity. It is generally acceptable that, in conducting a gyeorugi, a stance with a narrow base and a high position of the center of gravity is liable to be unstable, yet it is sometimes useful for a more powerful and speedier movement. From the viewpoint of functional relation, the *samgeuk* consisting of point, surface, and line, is the determinant factor, as a kinetic principle, to decide the speed and agility in executing a revolving movement, motions of translation, and others. It is possible, by making gyeorugi one of sports, to create a dynamic speed and rhythmical movements as well as to improve the function of movements through an understanding of the kinetic theory of the *yeokhak* principles in the *Han* philosophy.

3. The Principle of *Han* Philosophy

A human being is an entity making symbolic actions and he relies on a symbolic approach to the recognizing of an object. The thought of *samgeuk* consisting of heaven, earth, and human being can be expressed by the symbols of circle, square, and triangle (○, □, △). The practice of taekwondo is itself an application of the physical theory of *Han* philosophy and is aimed at acquiring a mastery of the system and nature of *han*, in which the triple essence, i.e., heaven, earth, and human being, is believed to be one. This system of three symbols constitutes the fundamentals of all movements related to taekwondo. The symbol of a circle meaning revolution is *gi* which makes one move, that of a square indicates the base representing a stance, and that of a triangle is the figurative shape of arms, representing a technique, and all the three combined into one make a complete movement, the so-called *pum*, according to the principle of oneness in the *Han* philosophy.

Going into more details, a circle is a universal symbol representing the entirety, perfection, simultaneity, and the completeness of an original. Platonists viewed a circle as a moving image of the immovable eternity, while Zenists saw a circle as a symbol of perception. A square, which can be contrasted with a circle symbolizing the heaven as the source of life and dynamic motions, represents the images of all the existence on the ground, static perfection, constancy, integration, and fixation. A square together with a circle are regarded as the symbols of the order of all things in the universe as well as the human world. In the meantime, a triangle represents a trinity of the universe, i.e., heaven/earth/ human being, and also father/mother/children, human flesh/soul/spirits, and a mystic figure of 3.

Taekwondo movements are comprised of the efficient techniques produced by an imitation of the shapes and postures of all things in the universe as well as their movements of contact and interaction, and they come from many of natural symbols to reflect the consistency between human beings and the universe. Even the Olympic motto of three words, faster, higher, and stronger, which are sought after as an ideal of Olympic sports, can be well applicable to the *yeokhak* principles of *Han* philosophy.

The geometrical diagrams (○, □, △) altogether have a philosophical meaning: a human being, the little universe as the subjective entity of *Han* philosophy, makes a unity with nature, the great universe. Throughout all the courses of taekwondo pumsaes, ranging from Pumsae Taegeuk as a starting point to Pumsae Ilyeo as the symbol of lucky signs for all things in the universe, one will experience the training of many movements in the dimension of the universe.

The daily training of taekwondo is a process (or a way) of accomplishing *han* as the principle of *Han* philosophy, which involves the theory of the universe.

Basic Movements

In making a series of movements to form a taekwondo technique, one starts with the first motion, which is called a basic movement. A movement is an intentional action to move the body as well as the hands and feet for offense and defense activities. This movement, as part of an individual technical movement of taekwondo, is classified into *poom* (static) and movement (mobile) in terms of its moving pattern.

Basic movements consist of 13 among various movements for offense and defense techniques: beginning with gibon junbi-seogi (basic ready stance), juchum-seogi momtong-jireugi (trunk-punching in riding stance), arae-makgi (blocking to defend the lower part of the body), momtong bandae-jireugi (trunk-punching with the opposite-side fist), ap-chagi (front kick), sonnal bakkat-chigi (hitting with the hand-blade from the outer side), momtong-makgi (blocking to defend the trunk), yeop-chagi (side kick), eolgul-makgi (blocking to defend the face), sonnal mok-chigi (hitting with the hand-blade at the neck), dollyeo-chagi (turning kick), momtong baro-jireugi (trunk-punching with the proper-side fist), and ending by returning to gibon junbi-seogi.

A movement is conducted by an integral functioning of all parts of the body, varying in forms according to the stance, the angle of the trunk, and the forms of the hand and foot. The composition of this specific movement follows the *Han* principle of circle, square, and triangle, which correspond respectively with the center of gravity (equilibrium), the vertical line of the center of gravity, and the base, as may be denoted by the symbols of point, line, and surface. They are the fundamental elements to frame various forms of offense and defense techniques.

This principle also applies to the variation of bodily movements, such as stability, movement of the center of gravity, flexibility, and intensity of power. The symbol of a point is itself a small circle, having different meanings according to its size. The point symbolizes a function as the center of gravity as well as a point of contact to convey power. On the other hand, a line can be classified into a horizontal line (base or surface) and a vertical line. The horizontal line stands for a stance (seogi) with which a man moves in a standing position, and the vertical line denotes the line crossing the center of gravity of the body. If the line of the center of gravity comes closer to the center of the base line, the body becomes more and more stable, and the high-low of the center of gravity affect the stability of a stance, and the flexibility and speed of a movement.

A movement is carried out in two different ways: counteraction and translation The two principles of movement are both applied to taekwondo techniques, which are mainly composed of makgi (blocking), jireugi (punching), jjireugi (thrusting or piercing), chigi (hitting), chagi (kicking), and others. For example, junbi-seogi, sonnal-makgi, etc. are conducted by motions of translation, while jireugi, arae-makgi, dollyeo-chagi, etc. by motions of counteraction. A motion of translation is carried out by attraction and a motion of counteraction by repulsive force; in both cases, the principle of yin-yang can be applied because the harmony between one hand and the other or between the hand and the foot creates the *gi* (the atmospheric force). A *gi* phenomenon can be created when the force centered around the *danjeon* (the abdomen) is spurted out from there to make motions of a movement almost unconsciously and flexibly due to the centrifugal nature of force. One may be able to make a movement of the body rhythmical and thereby control the intensity of *gi* and coordinate a motion of the body with breathing, if one faithfully abides by the rules of making basic movements.

At the time of training basic movements, in which one moves forward or retreats backward on the axis of the two feet, one must take a special heed to the foot acting as the principal axis regarding its direction as well as the moving of the center of gravity. Basic movements are the fundamentals of taekwondo, constituting the bases of the whole series of taekwondo techniques. Trainees of taekwondo must make incessant efforts to firmly grasp the principles of the basic movements or basic techniques, master the skills, and eventually implant them into the trainees themselves, even during the training of higher genres, such as pumsae and gyeorugi. Doing exercises of the body is the essential phenomenon of a human living.

Pumsae (Principle)

Pumsae is valued as a more important unit of training in taekwondo than gyeorugi and gyeokpa (breaking). The system of taekwondo techniques employing the hands and feet is in principle based on the *Han* philosophy, and each pum or movement of all those techniques implies a symbolic character of the triple essence, i.e., heaven, earth, and human being. A series of Pumsae Taegeuk (ranging from Jang 1 to Jang 8) are devised for Geup-grade trainees, and they are successively followed by Pumsaes Goryeo, Geumgang, Taebaek, Pyeongwon, Sipjin, Jitae, Cheongwon, Hansu, and finally by Pumsae Ilyeo, which are devised for the training of Dan black belts. All those pumsaes contain the color of Korean traditions and the thoughts of nature.

Lao-tse said, A human being learns from the earth, the earth from the heaven, the heaven from *do*, and *do* from nature which means being itself. In this way, the whole system of taekwondo techniques (earth) follows the principles of movement (heaven), the principles of movement follow the norms and laws of the pumsae-line, which is *do*, and then the pumsae-line takes its model after the thoughts of nature and Korean traditions.

The principle of pumsae can be explained by the principle of the art of self-defense in offense and defense activities from the viewpoint of techniques, by the *Han* philosophy from the philosophical viewpoint, and by the principle of dynamic-static arts from the viewpoint of arts.

First, all techniques or movements contained in a pumsae adopt the *ri-gi* principle in their functioning as an art of self-defense with offensive and defensive motions. In accordance with the variation of *ri* and *gi* a movement (or technique) becomes rapid or slow, strong or weak, and high or low.

Second, from the philosophical viewpoint, all movements of a pumsae contain the thought of *samgeuk*, that is, heaven, earth, and human being. Each movement follows the principles of *Han* philosophy because it applies the kinetic principles of a circle, square, triangle, point, line, and surface, which are geometrical symbols. All pumsaes are designed to represent their respective names and to follow the pumsae-lines philosophically signifying the cosmic structure, and, in reality, their training is a philosophical act of the entire body, performing conscious and repetitious, as well as figurative and symbolic, motions.

Third, from an artistic viewpoint, a pumsae applies the principle of dynamic-static art; therefore, artistic dynamics can be found in pums and movements. This principle makes a trainee of pumsae reach the stage of artistic ecstasy when he/she succeeds in bringing into a relationship of I and You (body and mind) all those natural, artistic, fantastic, and aesthetic feelings he or she experiences amidst an artistic atmosphere created by motions, variations, recurrences, and others. Pum is referred to as a static state, and a movement as a dynamic state; a combination of the two structures all kinds of techniques, which can manifest a dynamic art when they are performed in accordance with the principle of *ri* and *gi,* i.e., minds direction and bodys fulfillment.

The practice of taekwondo ultimately aims at perfecting a human being. In practicing pumsaes, one must always make efforts to understand all those principles and carry out a volitional, conscious, and repetitious training of the body, which will eventually lead one to an enriched human life.

Gyeorugi (Competition)

Gyeorugi, by its traditional meaning, is an application of a pumsae to combat against a real opponent; therefore, its training eyes mastering real fighting skills. This training course comes after a complete and repeated training of basic movements and pumsaes. The terminology gyeorugi is a noun form of gyeoruda (to compete with an opponent to win a victory) in Korean. The gyeorugi is classified into a coordinated gyeorugi, competition gyeorugi, and special gyeorugi. And, the coordinated gyeorugi is again divided into a onefold gyeorugi and a threefold gyeorugi. The competition gyeorugi is itself today's sports competition. The special gyeorugi involves an art of self-defense, requiring a high degree of difficulty in countering more than two opponents sometimes armed with weapons.

Through a hard training of gyeorugi, one can enhance self-confidence, fighting will, courage, spirit, and others, thereby enriching one's art of self-defense. In order to master gyeorugi skills, one must first have a good grasp of all determinant factors of gyeorugi, such as phase-by-phase changes of techniques, adjustment of a distance from the opponent, movements of the body, the selection of a target, and so on, and indulge oneself in repeating the training of them. One should also take heed to the observance of *ye* (courtesy) even in the practice of gyeorugi just as one did during the training of other units. The uttering of *gihap* (yelling with a concentration of spirit) is also an important factor that cannot be ignored during the practice of gyeorugi. An uttering of *gihap* implies a signal of starting a fight and is used as a means of concentrating *gi* and spirit.

When the attacker in gyeorugi pulls back the right foot and performs a oen-apgubi arae-makgi (blocking to defend the lower part in a left-hand forward-inflection stance) accompanied by a yell of *gihap*, it corresponds with yin according to the yin-yang principle. On the other hand, the defender yells a *gihap* at the same time that he performs a defense technique, which is considered to be an action of yang conducted in accordance with the kinetic principle of yin-yang philosophy.

A successful training of a defenders self-defense techniques can be achieved when the instructor arranges a careful organization and progressive guidance of training units so that changes may be made from an easy movement to a more difficult movement, and from a single movement to a complex and applied technique. Especially in the practice of gyeorugi, a trainee must always have it in mind that he should try to build up his body into a one under a total command of moral ethics through acquiring the skills well balanced between left and right, yin and yang, and *ri* and *gi*, following the principles applied to the composition of pumsaes.

In exercising his techniques, a defender must pay attention to such things as the sense of discriminating the situations, timing, control of *gi*, adjustment of the distance, *gihap*, etc., and choose the direction of progression by dodging, withdrawing, passing by, turning about, and others, always keeping in mind the center of gravity, the high and low of the target, and so on. All these derive from the application of the principles of *Han* philosophy. Taekwondo gyeorugi can be regarded as an application of practical philosophy because the contestants rely on the physical application of yin-yang and *ri-gi* as well as the metaphysical symbols of point, line, and surface, in countering and conquering their opponents by their own senses and *gi* (force), the instant they find weaknesses on the part of their opponents.

In this way, the philosophical ideas of the Korean race constitute the central concepts of taekwondo as well as its philosophical principles of motions.

Gyeokpa (Breaking)

Gyeokpa is one of the four key components of taekwondo training, following gyeorugi, pumsae, and basic movements, and it serves as a barometer to measure the intensity of power by means of breaking an object, mainly, pine boards, bricks, and roof tiles. In fact, gyeokpa is the best and comprehensive means to evaluate how powerful taekwondo techniques are; therefore, it is regarded as an engagement of real combat against an object by using bodily actions and as a personal experience of one's self. In general, taekwondo trainees are to undergo given tests during all courses of phase-by-phase training so that they may be evaluated to be qualified for gaining promotion to next higher Geup, Pum or Dan grades. However, noteworthy is that today there is a tendency to include gyeokpa as a mandatory one of the test subjects especially at dojangs, where the value of martial art taekwondo is more emphasized.

Gyeokpa is the best means to attract audiences attention with its powerful image at the time of tests or rehearsals at demonstration events, thereby motivating the audience to practice taekwondo. The essential quality of taekwondo lies in the satisfaction with the effect of training which trainees enjoy, when they personally experience the true value of martial arts by conducting a gyeokpa, which proves all joints of the body could be turned into weapons. Especially, a gyeokpa demonstration staged for the public provides a better chance, as a means of publicity, to show the audience what really taekwondo is like, sometimes arousing utterances of praising words like the divinely-skilled martial arts.

A gyeokpa can be executed in various fashions using either the hand or the foot or both: from simple to complex; from single to plural successive actions; and a mixture of movements by the hand and foot. Demonstration of some exquisite feats of high difficulty and display of formidable destructive power can be done by a gyeokpa. A conventional method of gyeokpa was mainly limited to the showing of destructive power only, but today the gyeokpa techniques have become diversified, including something like acrobatics, as the gyeokpa art came to be developed into an item of demonstration events for the interest of the public.

There have been painstaking efforts by experts to develop many highly difficult feats of gyeokpa through unceasing experiments and researches. Gyeokpa is an expression of bodily actions based on a practical philosophy, which can be realized in a state of unifying the body and mind, yin and yang, *ri* and *gi*, *che* (earth) and *yong* (heaven), metaphysics and physics, etc. In breaking an object , the gyeokpa technique applies the tripolar kinetic principles, e.g., heaven-earth-human being, circle-square-triangle, and point-surface-line. The heaven, circle, and point are corresponded with the original creation of power, i.e., *ri*, the sense, concentration of spirit, and the joint parts; the earth, square, and surface represent an object of breaking; and finally, the human being, triangle, and line mean speed, intensity of *gi* (force), angular motions, and others.

The true quality of gyeokpa lies in the unification of the body and mind, like the unity of *ri* (the sense, and concentration of spirit) and *gi* (force or power), or breathing (*ri*) and motion (*gi*), which are governed by the kinetic principle of *Han* philosophy, representing a tripolar unity of heaven, earth, and human being. In other words, all elements of gyeokpa technique, such as stance, angle, agility, distance, power of spirit, control of breathing and power, etc., on the part of the actor of gyeokpa (breaker), should follow the principle of *taegeuk*, which rules creation and variation, and the *ri-gi* principle of *Han* philosophy, the philosophical basis of the Korean people.

Art of Self-defense

In the series of taekwondo training, art of self-defense can be defined as a special technique in that it involves the application of all taekwondo techniques and takes the form of a real combat. The terminology of art of self-defense is mainly used in taekwondo, judo and others. The art of self-defense is naturally composed of those techniques which are intended to safeguard the body, necessarily with a focus on the movements facing an enemy, and are largely borrowed from offensive and defensive movements of martial arts.

An enemy or opponent may take an offensive act in two ways: either an attack with an item of weaponry in hand, such as a knife, club, and pistol; or a bare-handed attack without any weaponry, simply trying to grab or blow down the defender from all directions, front, back, or sides. The defender should react, according as the attacker moves, by keeping the place, withdrawing, advancing, passing by, or taking other motions, which all require a swift movement of the body.

In countering the opponents attack, applying the principle of power (*gi*) may differ according to the quality of the opponents power. When the atmosphere moves and changes, two qualities consist together, i.e., pulling and pushing. Likewise, art of self-defense, too, generally relies on the two qualities of pulling and pushing. In mass, there exist attraction and repulsion; however, the both eventually return to one force (*gi*) because the pulling force is tended to join the pushing force while the pushing force to join the pulling force.

Therefore, art of self-defense must be trained in such a manner as to keep a balance (homeokinesis) by means of harmonizing yin and yang depending on the intensity of the opponents power, the distance, and the speed. Here, the intensity, speed, and distance can be likened to the philosophical principles of point, line, and surface (or heaven-earth-human being), and the motion patterns of movements as well as the technical skills of bending, releasing, and finishing, may also apply the principles of *Han* philosophy.

Hapkido, a genre of self-defense arts, adopts the Three Great Principles of circle, flow, and harmony. All hapgido techniques including the technique of switching are employed according to the principle of a circle, and all movements are carried out by following the flow of power or by exploiting the flow of power. Lastly, harmony makes one move in concert with the opponents movement, thereby sparing his own strength and doubling the impact strength.

Special Qualities
of Pumsae

5

Special Qualities of Pumsaes

Pumsae

Pumsae is a major unit of training for taekwondo, containing the entire system of standard taekwondo techniques. Pumsaes, together with gyeorugi, gyeokpa, and self-defense art, are the typical genres of taekwondo training, and each genre enjoys a variety of functions. It is said, in the Gukgiwon-edited *Taekwondo Textbook*, that, from the technical point of view, pumsae is itself taekwondo because the basic movements are no more than the preliminary exercises preparing for the practice of pumsae, and gyeorugi is only an application of pumsae to a real fight or competition. Even the spirit of taekwondo can be found in the movements of pumsae themselves rather than in literal expressions of the symbolic and abstract mental philosophy.

Another definition of pumsae described that the training of pumsae provides the trainees with not only combat skills but an artistic delight, and it turns their interest in fighting into the pleasure of arts; therefore, pumsae can be defined as one of artistic forms. (Kim Dae-sik and others, eds., *The Taekwondo Textbook*). Pumsae, a pure Korean terminology, is a coumpound of *pum* and *sae*. *Pum* is an incomplete noun form, and, adding up to a verb, it denotes a certain movement, form, or character, while *sae* signifies a style, taste, appearance, and the like. In addition, *pum* has the meaning of a static state of a movement already suspended, and *sae* the meaning of a dynamic state of an entity. However, this terminology of *pumsae* was adopted only on February 26, 1987, by the Technical Council of Gukgiwon. Before that time, there had been denominations of *hyong* (form) and *pumse*.

The current patterns of pumsae were first formulated by an ad hoc committee (consisting of Lee Jong-wu and other 11 members) under the Researches Committee of the Korea Taekwondo Association. Then, on March 14, 1972, there was held a public hearing regarding the institution of pumsaes at the Grand Lecture Hall of the KTA on the 10th floor, with the participation of Han Hyong-sik, an official of the Ministry of Education, and provincial representatives of schools (Hyon Wu-yeong and other 8 persons), in addition to all members of the above-mentioned ad hoc committee for institution of pumsaes. After the hearing, an elaborate work for modification was done before the current pumsaes were finally fixed to be effective.

All pumsaes are equally characterized by three principles: the symmetrical disposition of movements on both left and right procession lines stemming from the main pumsae-line; a diverse and dynamic combination of movements at both the front and the back of the pumsae-line; and the consistency and recurrence of movements by beginning with a junbi-seogi (ready stance) and ending the pumsae also with a junbi-seogi. A pumsae is composed of the yin-yang principle deriving from the *Han* philosophy, the *samgeuk* principle of heaven, earth, and human being, and the principle of static-dynamic kinetics.

The yin-yang principle, as the fundamental principle of offense and defense techniques, is meant to produce an explosive power by the combination of skill (technique) and *gi* (force); the *samgeuk* principle, implying the *Han* philosophy, applies to the kinetic principles of cycling, line, and angle as depicted by geometrical diagrams of a circle, square, and triangle; and lastly the principle of static-dynamic kinetics represents an artistic value of aesthetic dynamics expressed in pums and other movements. A pum (form) implies a static state and a movement a dynamic state; therefore, all techniques can be expressed in rhythmical beauty out of extensive rhythms, in which the trainees can experience aesthetic tastes.

The training of pumsaes is aimed at experiencing the philosophical value of action art, which can be achieved by understanding the principle and spirit of *Han* philosophy latent in pumsaes and by practicing them repeatedly. The pumsae is a principal unit of taekwondo training, and accounts for 60 percent of the total rating points at Dan promotion tests. There are 25 patterns of pumsaes in all, of which 17 patterns except for 8 Palgwae pumsaes (Jang 1 to Jang 8) have been authorized to be trained all over the world. They are 8 Taegeuk Pumsaes (Jang 1 to Jang 8) for lower grades and 9 others for black belts, each having a specific name, Goryeo, Geumgang, Taebaek, Pyongwon, Sipjin, Jitae, Cheongwon, Hansu, and Ilyeo.

The Philosophy of Pumsae

The pumsae is defined as a mode of action expressing, directly or indirectly, the nourishment of mind and body as well as the offense and defense principles, with the movements comprising the essence of taekwondo spirit and techniques. The pumsae consists of a series of offensive and defensive techniques linking one after another in accordance with the fixed rules, so that the trainees may be able to practice them even without any guidance by an instructor. The pumsae-line means a line indicating the positions of the foot and the direction of its procession in carrying out a pumsae. (See the Gukgiwon-edited *Taekwondo Textbook*).

The pumsae is the nucleus of all taekwondo techniques and contains all principles, spirit, and virtues deriving from the *Han* philosophy of the Korean race; therefore, one should be aware that the taekwondo practice must not be simply limited to the physical dimension of mastering techniques but must be paralleled with the metaphysical dimension of polishing mind and body so that one may reach the stage of perceiving one's self. The pumsae is composed of the technical movements based on the principle of circle-square-triangle and the pumsae-line which follows the principle of point-line-surface; therefore, its training will lead one to an inner world governing philosophical and kinetic principles, i.e., the principles of *ri-gi*, yin-yang, and static-dynamic kinetics.

These symbols of circle-square-triangle and point-line-surface come from the symbolic concepts of the *Han* philosophy which mean heaven, earth, and human being. Makgi (blocking), jireugi (punching), chigi (hitting), and chagi (kicking) among the technical movements, and their targets, eolgul (face), momtong (trunk), and arae (the lower part), are well matched by an exquisite combination of *ri-gi*, yin-yang, and static-dynamic principles. Likewise, the pumsae-line is expressed in the geometrical diagrams of point, line, and surface, denoting the principles by a point, the center of gravity of the body by a line, and a spiritual world configured in the Korean people's philosophical thoughts by the surface.

The practice of pumsaes, which requires a lasting and repetitious training, is a systematic act intended to find out the true nature of a human being , i.e., the minds *ri*, from the inner world of spirit characterized by the 4 dispositions of mind (benevolence, righteousness, courtesy, and wisdom) and the 7 emotions (delight, anger, sorrow, pleasure, love, vice, and avarice), which are the central ideas of Scholar Toegye. Therefore, it constitutes a process of perfecting ones self to embody the virtues of benevolence, righteousness, courtesy, and wisdom, as well as to refine the mind, human nature, and emotions. The practice of pumsaes is an act of recognizing ones self, thinking and reflecting on oneself, and personally experiencing ones true life.

If taekwondo practitioners keep themselves always cognizant, during the course of pumsae training, that the spiritual world of human beings will eventually become the more luminous, and the life of human beings the more bright, then the practitioners will get imbued with the aesthetic sensibility, finally to make their surroundings look more beautiful. The more we reflect on ourselves in our life, the more we will become righteous with an ethical mind and the more deeply we will experience our spiritual world. The moral consciousness, in its quality as the light of existence, makes the world open up to us bright and helps a human being evolve into a self-reflecting and liberal one.

The inner life of a human being, through the polishing of his self, can formulate an inner world, in which he leads a new life of his own. Especially, the inner world of taekwondo spirit is full of the spirit of the Korean race, which has long been cultivated in the midst of all lives with common living styles and common emotions, sharing the fate and lot as well as joys and sorrows among the people themselves. And, this inner world can be attained by the practice of pumsae, the essence of taekwondo, which can be freely practiced by whoever, whenever and wherever.

Practicing pumsaes does not mean a mere acquisition of skills in technical movements, but an experience of an all-around person, unifying all that is intellectual, moral, aesthetic, and philosophical. We begin and end with bowing in an expression of courtesy to practice pumsaes, and, during all the course of training, we undergo a metaphysical training of the inner world based on the *Han* philosophy of heaven, earth, and human being, as well as a physical training to acquire techniques, all of which are aimed at developing ourselves into integral and complete selves, i.e., all-around persons. These philosophical activities unceasingly repeated for self cultivation are exactly what pumsaes are designed to encourage, which, in other words, is the very philosophy of pumsae leading to the ultimate objective of reaching a *do*.

Pumsae-line

The pumsae-line is the way of a pumsae, indicating a pattern to symbolize the idea the pumsae is designed to seek. If the process of movements, in which all pumsaes are framed, created, and changed by the combination of defense and offense techniques, is analogized with nature, the pumsae-line is like the cosmos which acts as a principle to move the nature.

As for Pumsae Taegeuk, it derives from the principles of yin-yang and the five elements of the universe, which constitute the bases of the Korean peoples philosophy, because *taegeuk* is believed to be the origin of the universe to govern the principle of yin-yang (expressed in symbols of -- and —) as represented by earth and heaven, water and fire, and others, and the *gi* phenomenon of *taegeuk* creates lightening, wind, mountain, sun, moon, stars, and others. The symbol of yin is delineated by a long bar, (—), one of the divination signs, and that of yang by two short bars (a division of that long bar); therefore, the *Han* philosophy implies that one comprises all, i.e., one in two parts, one that is large, many, and so on.

The *Han* philosophy views that nature and a human being are in the relationship of infinity comprising limits, which may be applied to the relationship between pumsae and pumsae-line. The subject governing a pumsae-line is a human being. The human being, who acts in accordance with the principles of yin-yang and the five elements of the universe, fulfills the laws (pumsae) according to the order (pumsae-line) by means of governing all movements of the main entity, which are carried out in the unity of *che* (body) and *yong* (employment), mind and body, spirit and motion, etc., so that they may be developed into philosophical, somatologic, and aesthetic movements.

The pumsae-line starts by an expression of courtesy, progresses in the form of the yin-yang symmetry and balance between the movements on the left and the right, passing through the three phases of *taegeuk* representing heaven, earth, human being, and finally returns to the starting point also with an expression of courtesy.

Pumsae Taegeuk is the training course for beginners and Geup-grade trainees in that it implies the principles of the creation of the universe as well as the norms of human life. Pumsae Taegeuk begins with Jang (field) 1, symbolizing the heaven, and ends with Jang 8, symbolizing the earth. For black belts, the pumsae begins with Pumsae Goryeo, whose pumsae-line symbolizing the martial arts spirit, and ends with Pumsae Ilyeo, whose pumsae-line signifying the return to one or *han*.

Pumsae-lines contain all thoughts and ideas of the Korean race, ranging from the ideal of *hongik-ingan* to the thought of *sipjangsaeng* (10 creatures of long life), and, in the end, include the Ilyeo thought represented by the martial arts philosophy based on the *pungryu* thoughts, which focus on nature and yet lay importance on the true nature of a human being. A pumsae-line, involving all principles of *ri-gi*, static-dynamic, yin-yang, and the five elements, is a field on which to conduct physical actions to attain the perception of *do* during the process of displaying the *gi* latent in a human being or going into a world of *ri* beyond that world of *gi*.

Different Patterns of Pumsae-lines

Pumsae Taegeuk : consists of 8 Jangs, representing 8 *gwes* (divination signs) of the Oriental philosophy of the Book of Changes (*juyeok*), roughly taking the shape of a Chinese character, '王', signifying a king.

Pumsae Goryeo : takes the form of a Chinese character '士', signifying a scholar.

Pumsae Geumgang : takes the form of a Chinese character '山', signifying a mountain.

Pumsae Taebaek : takes the form of a Chinese character '工', signifying construction.

Pumsae Pyongwon : takes the form of a Chinese character '一', signifying one.

Pumsae Sipjin : takes the form of a Chinese character '十', signifying ten.

Pumsae Jitae : takes the form of a vowel 'ㅗ' (o) of the Korean alphabet.

Pumsae Cheongwon : takes the form of a vowel 'ㅜ' (u) of the Korean alphabet.

Pumsae Hansu : takes the form of a Chinese character '水', signifying water.

Pumsae Ilyeo : takes the form of a swastika, the symbol of Buddhism '卍'.

Junbi-seogi (Ready Stance)

The junbi-seogi is a symbolic stance to be taken, along with a bow in expression of courtesy, at the beginning and at the end of training such movements as the basic movements, pumsaes, coordinated gyeorugi, gyeorugi, and others. The junbi-seogi, which belongs to the category of a special pum stance, comprises gibon (basic) junbi-seogi, *tongmilgi* (pushing-hands ready stance), gyeopson (overlapped-hands ready stance), bojumeok (covered-fist ready stance), and gyeorumsae (competition stance). Generally, the gibon junbi-seogi and the gyeorumsae are the most frequently used.

To form a gibon junbi-seogi, you stand in a parallel stance and bring two fists side by side in front of the abdomen, concentrating *gi* (the atmospheric force), the center of gravity, and the spirit on one point. In this stance, a triangle is formed with the face at the top and two fists and two feet, symbolizing a man. In a gibon junbi-seogi, the left foot moves on the axis of the right foot (yang), while, in a gyeorumsae, the right foot moves on the axis of the left foot (yin). This is because the junbi-seogi usually focuses on makgi (blocking) techniques during the training of martial arts taekwondo, while gyeorugi is trained for competitions, which require more offensive tactics.

In posing a junbi-seogi, you must make stabilized movements, controlling the breathing to bring the force, spirit, and the direction of your eyes into harmony. The junbi-seogi is the basic form of all other special-pum stances, keeping the arms, feet, and the trunk in harmony for their movements. As for the tongmilgi junbi-seogi, you stand first in a naranhi-seogi (parallel stance), and keep the hands open to make their palms look each other, slowly lift the hands upward from the lower abdomen to the level of the lower part of the face via the solar plexus, and finally fix the palms as if holding a circle (like a volley-ball), metaphysically representing the heaven. This symbol of a circle may render the trainees a metaphysical image to remind the order and harmony of all things in the universe.

On the other hand, the gyeopson junbi-seogi, starting from a moa-seogi (close stance), keeps the left hand palm overlapping the back of the right hand palm to make the shape of an emblem of *taegeuk* or yin-yang. Two palms making a *taegeuk* emblem give out an image of praying as a sign of thinking always of the heaven. Also the bojumeok (covered-fist) junbi-seogi starts from a close stance, and makes the left hand palm (yin) lightly cover the right hand fist (yang), the supporting forearms forming a triangle to signify a human being.

The forms of all junbi-seogis are characterized by the emphasis on a metaphysical thinking of nature, reminding the trainees of the necessity to adapt themselves to the order of and fuse themselves with nature. They also stress the need to contemplate the order and philosophical principles of the universe as well as the spiritual and ideological world of a human being.

Chaper **6** *six*

Gyeorugi as an Olympic Sport

6

Gyeorugi as an Olympic Sport

The Philosophy of Gyeorugi

Gyeorugi has now been fixed as one of the competition sports, being an independent genre of taekwondo. As a competition sport, gyeorugi can be performed on a square mat 12m x 12m wide, where two competitors, Blue and Red, confront each other to win a victory by supremacy of technical abilities during the contest of 3 rounds of 3 minutes each.

From the viewpoint of Oriental philosophies, the mat called "the contest area" can be likened to the globe (earth), and the number 3 (rounds) represents the universe consisting of space and time according to the triple essence of Han philosophy symbolizing heaven, earth, and human being. On the other hand, the contestants, Red and Blue, signifying yin-yang, as well as the round scoring areas marked on the protector are likened to space, while the 3 minutes to time. If the competition rules are like the cosmic order, all the movements unceasingly undertaken by the contestants to gain scores may be likened to the cosmic operation, in which to seek the best way to harmonize all philosophical principles, such as *ri-gi*, yin-yang, the five elements of the universe, and the Confucian five cardinal virtues.

The requirements for a contestant to win a competition is his superior competition abilities. From the viewpoint of the kinetic theory, the competition ability means a contestant's abilities to carry out a contest, which can be generally referred to a synthesis of such factors as physical strength, skill, tactics, and competition spirit. Physical strength is meant by the bodily strength to act, which may differ more or less depending on the type of competition. However, physical strength is the ability displayed by a bodily technique in the midst of activities by the body, and it is usually governed by the active motor organs. Therefore, physical strength comprises both energy-related factors, such as muscular strength, speed, automatic-response power, and endurance, and factors of power controlling, such as adaptability, equilibrium, flexibility, and agility.

The techniques of gyeorugi are mainly borrowed from the traditional technical system of taekwondo, notably, kicking, punching, stepping (jitgi), and others. And, the competition spirit is meant by the power of spirit or power of concentration governing a persistent endurance and self-restraint. After all, the competition ability corresponds with the principles of yin-yang and the five elements of the universe as well as the Confucian five cardinal virtues (benevolence, justice, politeness, wisdom, and fidelity) in the eyes of the Oriental philosophers. A contest between two players of yin and yang (Blue and Red) is conducted according to the competition rules, i.e., the cosmic order, with fierce exchanges of yang and yin techniques, e.g., kicking vs. counter-kicking and attack vs. counterattack. The five elements of the universe imply speed by fire, flexibility and rhythm by water, agility and automatic-response power by wood, endurance and physical strength by metal, and technique and tactics by earth, which are the forces and actions to create all things (scoring by attack techniques) in the heaven and earth (the competition area).

In the meantime, the Confucian five cardinal virtues, which are the true natures of a human being, can be explained as follows:

Benevolence implies the ability to acquire and exercise all skills; justice an adamant offensive capability; politeness the spirit of fair play; wisdom the ability to choose either an offensive or a defensive, and to choose a target, an applicable technique, and tactics; and fidelity implies self-confidence, and the power of spirit or power of concentration.

It is an act of doing a justice to do one's best to protect "benevolence" during the engagement of a gyeorugi. This exactly means "doing an act of benevolence at the sacrifice of oneself." At the time of starting and ending a contest, the players bow toward each other, which is the expression of politeness to pay their respects to others as well as to themselves. By "wisdom," the players make a correct moral estimate of the situations, and also, by "fidelity," they rely on their insight and moral freedom. To abide by the competition rules and to show the spirit of fair play are the acts of practical philosophy aimed at achieving their unity with the universe by means of observing the cosmic order and fiercely rivaling in a struggle to transcend the limits of human accomplishments.

Gyeorugi as a competition sport, based on the above-mentioned five virtues, is indeed the process of attaining the maximum level of competition ability in conformity with the fundamental nature of a human being and, at the same time, is an act of cultivating oneself with all those virtues in the course of performing moral conducts during a contest.

From the viewpoint of the Oriental philosophies, the competition ability of gyeorugi as defined by the Western kinetics can be interpreted as the spirit of five virtues, which is the essence of gyeorugi and with which we hope to recover the true human nature. The philosophy of gyeorugi lies in experiencing the entire process of conducting moral acts and embodying the true nature of a human being, which can be achieved: first by making all our efforts to exert the maximum competition ability (the nature of five virtues); by accomplishing the five virtues through moral acts of a fair play; by demonstrating the spirit of overcoming all hardships in exploring our own life (becoming champions) and the world; and finally by attaining the perfection of ourselves.

Gyeorumsae

Gyeorumsae is an abridged form of words meaning a gyeorugi stance, defined as the standard stance the two contestants take during the process of gyeorugi. When the two contestants face each other, they take either a "yeollimsae" (opened gyeorugi stance) or "dachimsae" (closed gyeorugi stance) depending on the formation of facing each other. The yeollimsae refers to the formation, in which the target of attack is opened to the opponent; in other words, both contestants put forth a foot on their different side, for example, the contestant Blue the right foot and the Red the left foot. On the other hand, the dachimsae formation is made when the target of attack is closed or hidden to each other; for instance, the Blue and the Red put forth their foot on the same side.

The gyeorumsae is the basic posture to facilitate the movements of attack or blocking and closely related with the skillfulness of techniques leading to an attack or a blocking. Players must try hard to master a correct stance even in the stage of basic training, so that they may easily move their bodies. Especially, the balance of the body and the agility of bodily movements depend a large part on how the gyeorumsae is taken.

The types of gyeorumsae are generally classified into 3 patterns according to the posture taken by a contesttant in the midst of gyeorugi or training.

(1) Gyeorumsae : this may also be called a front gyeorumsae, and is the standard pattern for all other gyeorumsaes.
(2) Yeop-gyeorumsae (side gyeorumsae) : this is a variation of the standard gyeorumsae, simply keeping the body sideways.
(3) Nachumsae (low gyeorumsae) : this is also a variation of the standard gyeorumsae, and this keeps the knees bent low and the body slightly looking sideways. The upper body may slightly lean forward.

The above 3 patterns are the most frequently observed during contests. However, players sometimes use many variations of gyeorumsae according as tactics requires. And, players must pay attention to the "jitgi" (step or footwork) and the choice of techniques to apply according to the type of gyeorumsae.

The preconditions for an ideal gyeorumsae are generally as follows:
■ Flexibility in all movements is mandatory.

- Agility must be exerted to the maximum in all movements.
- The base and the center of gravity must be adequately proportioned to keep the balance of the body.
- The efficiency of offense and defense techniques must be enhanced by moving the weight of the body.

Jitgi (step or footwork)

The main components of gyeorugi techniques are jumeok jireugi (fist punch), bal chagi (foot kick), feint motions, and jitgi (step). Punch and kick are direct techniques, and feint motions and step are indirect techniques.

"Jitgi" is an equivalent to the English word "step." The "step" in English literally has various meanings, such as stepping, distance of a step, pace, manner of walking, style of walking, way of stepping, etc., as a noun, and, as a verb, to tread on the foot (while dancing), and others. Originally, the word "step" meant a unit of the foot movement in dancing, i.e., a movement of a foot advancing forward to move the weight of the body. Therefore, this word has been gradually fixed to be a kind of basic technique in boxing and fencing sports. Then, it has also been adopted as a basic technique of taekwondo gyeorugi since the latter part of the 1980s as gyeorugi became an independent genre of taekwondo as a sport of games. In the boxing sport, the term of step, as a kind of footwork, means "to advance," "to put forth a foot, keeping balance of the body without breaking the stance of attack or blocking," and, especially, "to advance a foot powerfully a step forward at the time of delivering a stroke."

Attempts have been made to define a Korean version of the terminology of step used for gyeorugi, independently by several taekwondo experts, namely, Lee Seung-guk (1986), Choi Yeong-ryeol (1989), Kim Yeong-in (1991), and Kim Se-hyeok and the writer of this paper (see Bareun Taekwondo Gyobon, Tongmun-gwan, 1987). There were diverse definitions among those experts: Lee Seung-guk, Choi Yeong-ryeol, Kim Young-in, and others maintained that the word "step" should be adopted as it is, and Kim Se-hyeok, in his doctoral dissertation, used the term balnollim (moving of the foot). However, this writer has been continuously using the term jitgi.

We can find two words, baljit and baljil in the Korean dictionary. Baljil means an act of kicking with the foot, and baljit means simply an act of moving the foot, according to the dictionary. Therefore, this writer has found it proper to use the terminology of jitgi, a noun form, borrowed from a verb, baljit-hada (make motions of the foot), excluding the syllable bal which corresponds with the foot because taekwondo has already adopted an official terminology of chagi, a synonym of baljil (foot kick).

The step as a gyeorugi technique plays many important roles: the key role in coordinating the timing of a foot kick; a determinant role to weaken or blunt the opponent's attacking force; and, if required, the role of curbing in advance the delivery of an attack by the opponent. (See Choi Yeong-ryeol, A Theroy of Taekwondo Gyeorugi, Samhak Press, 1989). In taekwondo competitions, a step (or stepping) serves as an important defense technique and, at the same time, as a preliminary technique introducing an effective attack. (See Son Cheon-taek and another, Taekwondo Vol. 84, p. 58.).

It is unreasonable to include feinting and jumping in the category of jitgi (hereafter referring to the word "step"). Feinting is itself an independent technique of gyeorugi because it is a motion of deceiving the opponent to find an opportunity to attack, and jumping is simply an act of making the body bounce up from the ground for the purpose of exercising a technique. Techniques should be assorted logically and broken down simply for assurance of the maximum effect of training. Jitgi is a means of facilitating offense and defense activities by moving the center of gravity on one foot or both feet, thereby belonging to the category of indirect techniques.

The types of jitgi are classified, according to the movement direction of the feet, into naga-jitgi (advance step), mulleo-jitgi (reverse step), and bikyeo-jitgi (sidestepping step), and, according to the change in foot positions, into kkeureo-jitgi (closing-up step), dora-jitgi (turnaround step), and others.

Classification and methods of competition

1. Competition divided as follows :
   1) Individual competition shall normally be between comtestants in the same weight class. When nessary, adjoining weight classes may be combined to create a single classification.
   2) Team Competition
2. Systems of competitin are divided as follows :
   1) Single elimination tournament system
   2) Round robin system
3. All international level competitions recognized by the WTF shall be formed with participation of at least 3 countries with no less than 3 contestants in each weight class, and any weight class with less than 3 contestants cannot be recognized in the official results.

Competition area

The Competition Area shall measure 12m×12m in Metric system and have a flat surface without any obstructing projections.

The Competition Area shall be covered with an elastic mat.

However, the competition area may be installed on a platform 50cm-60cm high from the base, if necessary, and the outer part of the Boundary Line shall be inclined with a gradient of less than 30 degrees for the safrty of the contestants.

Demarcation of the competition area

1) The 8m×8m area in the inner part of the Competition Area of 12m

$\times$ 12m shall be called the Contest Area the outer part of the Contest Area shall be called the Alert Area.

2) The demarcation of the Contest Area and Alert Area shall be distinguished by the different colors of the two area's surface, or indicated by a white line 5cm wide when the entire surface is one color.

3) The demarcating line between the Contest Area and the Alert Area shall be called the Alert Line and the marginal line of the Competition Area shall be called the Boundary Line.

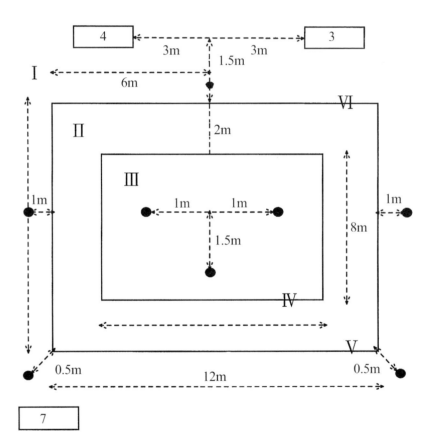

2-1

Ⅰ. Competition Area

Ⅱ. Alert Area

Ⅲ. Contest Area

Ⅳ. Alert Line

Ⅴ. Boundary Line

Ⅴ-1. 1st Boundary Line

   2nd, 3rd, and 4th Boundary

   Lines clockwise.

1. Referee's Mark

2. Judge's Mark

3. Recorder's Mark

4. Commission Doctor's Mark

5-1. Blue Contestant's Mark

5-2. Red Contestant's Mark

6-1. Blue Coach's Mark

6-2. Red Coach's Mark

7. Inspection Desk

Principles of scoring

1) Principles of independent decision making : The Referee must always make decisions based on his/her own judgement, independent of the influence of other Referee's decisions.

2) Priciples of immediate decision making : The Referee should make immediate decision regarding actions and must not hesitate to judge individuals techniques by, for instance, judging a combined technical sequence or Summing the context of technical actions. The Referee must make a judgement immediately after the action occurs.

3) Principle of non-compensation of misjudgement : If the Referee recognizes that he/she has made a misjudgement, he must not try to compensate by making another misjudgement.

   For example, when a Referee recognizes that he has penalized a contestant unreasonably, there is the tendency to try to compensate the mistake by penalizing the other contestant unreasonably or upon the slightest pre-text. This is a clear violation of rules and can be the cause of loss of dignity and credibility.

4) Principle of non-reevaluation of a previous judgement.

   Once a decision is made it must not be changed under any circumstance The only legal course of changing decisions is through arbitration.

Gukgiwon, Mecca of Taekwondo

7

Gukgiwon, Mecca of Taekwondo

The Logo of Gukgiwon

The current logotype of Gukgiwon has been put into effect as of February 1, 1976, after a modification of the original one. Lee Jong-wu, vice president of the WTF, personally designed this logotype, taking into consideration some philosophical principles: the logo as a whole expresses the idea that one can fully understand and master the natural order of the universe with a unity among self, other, and all things in conformity with the principle of *samjae*, i.e., heaven, earth, and human being. The inner circle representing the globe contains two figures in a *santeul-makgi* (wide-open or mountain blocking) stance, who try to bring about peace and solidarity for all human beings of different races and tongues in the world to form one family. This symbolizes the progressive spirit of human beings always looking upon the whole world. It also bears the inscriptions of Gukgiwon both in Korean and English, and World Taekwondo Headquarters in English.

Black Belt Promotion Tests and Issuance of Dan Certificates

An official event for Dan promotion tests was for the first time organized by the Korea Taekwondo Association on November 11, 1962, and, ever since, the KTA continued to maintain the authority of conducting promotion tests and issuing certificates until 1979. However, the general assembly of the KTA delegates on December 28, 1979, decided that all administrative affairs related to Dan promotion tests and issuance of certificates be transferred to the Gukgiwon as of February 5, 1980.

As of the end of 1998, the number of black belts registered at Gukgiwon counts more than 4 million throughout the whole world. And, the Gukgiwon now has grown to firmly secure the status as a nominal and real world taekwondo center, controlling all administrative works for the development of taekwondo in collaboration with the World Taekwondo Federation. The Gukgiwon has the objective, as its statute provides, to develop and disseminate taekwondo, the traditional cultural heritage of Korea, through a pan-national campaign, to improve the entire peoples fitness and arouse in them a sound and cheerful disposition, and then to diffuse the traditional spirit and techniques of taekwondo all over the world with a view to enhancing the national prestige and contributing to the development of the national culture.

Promotion tests for Geup grades are conducted at each dojang (gymnasium or club) under the superintendence of a master instructor who holds the instructors license, and promotion tests for Pum and Dan grades up to 5th Dan are commissioned to each city or provincial chapter of the KTA. Promotion tests for 6th Dan and over are only administered directly by the Gukgiwon. In case of the applicants in foreign countries, only the master instructors holding Gukgiwon Dan certificates of 4th Dan and over are authorized to conduct promotion tests. However, the Gukgiwon collects the applications of overseas testees to refer them to the Gukgiwon Promotion Test Commission, which screens and decides whether or not each of them can be qualified for a next higher grade. The Test Commission meets twice every month. However, those overseas applications from the countries belonging to Group 1 category must be accompanied by the recommendation of the president of Taekwondo Association the applicants are affiliated with.

The Gukgiwon Promotion Test Regulations have been revised on 7 occasions ever since it was first instituted by the KTA on March 1, 1972.

For overseas applications for 8th and 9th Dan promotion, the Gukgiwon invites the applicants, without an exception, to Gukgiwon, where they must personally undergo technical tests. In the meanwhile, the Gukgiwon has endeavored to improve a computerized data processing work, and on November 4, 1996, commissioned to the Samsung Data System the project of developing a new information system, thereby increasing the capacity of issuing Dan certificates from formerly around 1,000 copies to more than 4,000 copies a day.

The Government-authorized World Taekwondo Academy

The Taekwondo Academy, which is an additional institution to the Gukgiwon, had been conducting, beginning in February 1972, the program of training master instructors/coaches of taekwondo under the supervision of the KTA, until November 1, 1976, when the training began to be carried out at Gukgiwon.

In fact, it was the 28th class of 1980 that began to get the training under the direct management of the Gukgiwon, and it was only on November 29, 1983, that the Taekwondo Coaches Academy was officially recognized by the government as a government-authorized institution, thus formalizing a course for national coaches of taekwondo to obtain national licenses of Class-II coaches (in accordance with Art. 22-2 of the Enforcement Ordinance for the National Physical Education Promotion Law).

Again, in February 1990, the Ministry of Culture and Sports approved another course of training with the appellation of Sports-for-all Coaches Academy, which allows the issuance of licenses for Class-III sports-for-all coaches. Therefore, the Taekwondo Academy now administers 3 different courses, separately or in combination, training master instructors, coaches, and sports-for-all coaches. Those who complete the 9-day training course and pass the given test will obtain their instructors licenses as well as Class-III sports-for-all coach licenses, so that they may be qualified to open their own dojangs (gymnasiums).

Starting from the 72nd class of instructors course, an additional training for sports-for-all coaches (more than 60 hours) was integrated into the main course. This integral course has been maintained until the 105th class in 1999, and its major units of training consist of the theory of sports-for-all, the role and mission of sports instructors, the status quo of the Gukgiwon, kinetic physiology, training methods, sports psychology, sports social science, the theory on recreation, first aid and safety control, theories and practical practice of taekwondo, and others. The number of trainees who completed various courses of Taekwondo Academy has risen to over 26,000 persons up to the present (1998).

The English denomination of International Taekwondo Academy of Gukgiwon has been altered to the World Taekwondo Academy since 1996, with a view to matching the World Taekwondo Headquarters of Gukgiwon.

Taekwondo Museum (A Memorial Hall)

Taekwondo Museum was opened on November 30, 1991, the day of the 19th anniversary of the founding of Gukgiwon. Participating in this historic opening ceremony were Gukgiwon President Kim Un-yong, U.S. Taekwondo Union President An Gyeong-won, Jewoo Trading Co. President Kim Hyon-woo, and other leading taekwondo personalities, counting more than 150, who cut the tape, attracting the public interest. A variety of commemorative materials including various data files related to taekwondo are exhibited in Taekwondo Museum, which deserves a space of culture where one can well appreciate a vivid history of taekwondo. A lot of materials and items collected by Gukgiwon President Kim during all his activities as an IOC member are also exhibited there and this taekwondo memorial hall, as it is generally called at present, will become a real taekwondo museum in the future.

Visitors of this museum or hall since its opening counted by 1998 more than 50,000 personages, including IOC President Samaranch, IOC

Executive Board members, GAISF President Thomas Kelly, foreign ambassadors, and other domestic and foreign dignitaries, aside from many overseas taekwondo practitioners. This Taekwondo Museum, now a memorial hall, is located at the backyard of Gukgiwon on the 2nd floor of a quonset building, covering an area of 50 pyong. Its construction was completed in a year and 10 months after the plan was drawn up in February 1990, costing 50 million won.

The breakdown of all exhibited items is as follows : 346 pieces of framed pictures and posters, 40 trophies, 155 medals, 147 commemorative plaques, 270 memorial articles, over 400 pieces of video-tapes and films(concerning taekwondo games, Olympic Games held in Seoul, etc.), 171 taekwondo-related magazines, 28 files of newspaper articles related to taekwondo, 30 files of other newspaper articles, 250 taekwondo-related books, 335 sports-related books, and others.

This memorial hall is also equipped with a multi-video system, with which one can survey competition scenes of major international tournaments at any time he wants to, and in the hall, one can also find the photos of all winners of the past world championships, including the photo of Player Chung Kuk-hyun, who appears in the *Guinness Book of World Records* for his winning of 4-time champion as well as Chungs memorial items, such as uniform (dobok), girdle, and others, worn at the time of his championship contests.

Chaper 8 Eight

The World Taekwondo Federation

8

The World Taekwondo Federation (WTF)

The Background of Founding the WTF

In his inaugural address, Kim Un-yong, the 7th president of the Korea Taekwondo Association, made it public that Gukgiwon would be built as a central dojang for all taekwondo practitioners throughout the world. KTA President Kim had it in mind that Gukgiwon, as a mecca of world taekwondo, would serve as the place to host international competitions in order to develop taekwondo into an international sport. This was one of his commitments before he took office as the KTA president, and the first commitment was fulfilled when the construction of Gukgiwon was completed on November 30, 1972.

He always emphasized that the task of internationalizing taekwondo could be fulfilled by taking the leadership not only in technical supremacy but also in controlling relevant organizations.

For that purpose, he stressed, this country must organize world taekwondo championships, which may enable the country to be honored as the native land of taekwondo, to enhance the national prestige through a world-wide dissemination of the national martial arts taekwondo, to improve taekwondo techniques, and finally to promote strong ties among nations by establishing a system and order of international society based on the orthodox taekwondo philosophy.

As a result, the KTA planned to organize the 1st World Taekwondo Championships at Gukgiwon for 3 days from 25 to 27 of May 1973, sending invitations to 22 countries, namely, the United States, Japan, Germany, Austria, Canada, Great Britain, Malaysia, Thailand, Italy, Spain,

Turkey, Colombia, Ivory Coast, Philippines, Ecuador, Taipei, France, Guam Islands, Brazil, Hong Kong, Singapore, and Vietnam.

The Founding of the WTF

Prior to the inaugural general meeting of the World Taekwondo Federation, there was held a meeting of promoters at Gukgiwon at 13:00 hrs on May 27, 1973. Participating in this meeting were 9 persons from 6 countries: Korea (Kim Un-yong), U.S. (Jack Hwang and Edward B. Shell), Mexico (Romiro Osmin and Jose Torres Navarrette), Uganda (J.A.A. Etima), Taipei (Zi Jian-hong), Austria (Lee Kyong-myong and Georg Matuszek). The inaugural general meeting held on May 28 at Gukgiwon had 35 participants from 17 countries (Colombia, Philippines, Japan (Korean residents in Japan), Hong Kong, Guatemala, Taipei, U.S., Khmer (now Cambodia), Mexico, Ivory Coast, Malaysia, Austria, Singapore, Korea, Germany, Uganda, and Brunei).

Following the order of agenda, the general meeting proceeded under the chairmanship of Lee Jong-wu, now vice-president of the WTF, and, in the midst of a debate on the draft WTF Regulations, there arose an argument of pro and con regarding Article 4 Sec. 3, providing, The Federation authorizes the membership to only one organization for each country and autonomous territory. However, this provision was approved as it was by a majority of votes, i.e., 11 for and 5 against. In the election of officials, KTA President Kim Un-yong was unanimously approved to become the first president of the WTF, who was entrusted to appoint the remaining officials.

The inaugural general meeting adopted the WTF Rules and Regulations, ranging 18 articles, and decided that the 2nd World Taekwondo Championships will be held again in Seoul in 1975. In the meantime, there was a proposal by the Singapore delegate that an Asian taekwondo championships be held in Australia in 1974; however, the decision of the matter was commissioned to the executive committee to be formed. And, the selection of key WTF officials for a 4-year term, such as 3 vice-presidents, secretary general, and a small number of executive committee members, was also entrusted to the president.

Composition of the First-term Executive Body

WTF President Kim Un-yong on July 5, 1973, announced that he designated 3 WTF vice presidents, Secretary General, and 19 Executive Council members (including 4 members of right), and that the 1st Asian Taekwondo Championships would be held in Seoul in May 1974 prior to the 2nd World Taekwondo Championships, scheduled for 1975, and efforts would be made to include taekwondo in the official programs of the 8th Asian Games slated for 1978.

The members of the First Executive Body with a 4-year term of office were as follows :

Vice Presidents : Roland de Marco (USA), Leo Wagner (Germany), Kim Myong-hoe (Korea),

Secretary General : Lee Jong-wu (Korea)

Executive Council members : John M. Murphy (USA), Marx Heinz (Germany), Torres Navarrette(Mexido), Ungker Najardin (Malaysia), J. A. Etima (Uganda), Zhang Wei Guo (Taipei), L. Lacoste (France), Chiat Uskhan (Turkey), Park Keon-sok, Park Mu-seung, Roh Byong-jik, Uhm Woon-kyu, Lee Nam-sok, Hong Chong-soo (all from Korea), and Tang Chi Yuen (singapore)

The 1st International Referee Seminar

The First IR Seminar was held at Gukgiwon during May 15-18, 1974. Participants were 45 taekwondo coaches from 10 countries, of whom 31 passed the final exam. Participating countries were the United States (9 coaches), Germany (4), Chinese Taipei (4), Uganda (2), Guam (2), Turkey (2), Netherlands (1), Austria (1), France (1), and Korea (19).

Major topics of seminar consisted of Referees Attitudes (Lecturer Bae Young-ki), Refereeing Rules (by Lee Kyo-yoon), Methods of Marking Scores, Practice of Refereeing, and others.

The WTF so far has conducted 37 (by 1998) IR seminars, changing the location from one country to another, and 25 IR Refresher Courses, thus producing over 1,200 International Referees.

Various Types of Rules and Regulations

The WTF has amended its Rules and Regulations 11 times since its enactment on May 28, 1973, the Competition Rules 7 times since the same day, and has first enacted on August 17, 1993, the Regulations on the Organization and Operation/Management of Competitions. It also provided the IR Management Regulations on August 17, 1993 (one time amendment thereafter), the Regulations on Disciplinary Sanctions on August 17, 1993, and the Regulations on Doping Tests of Prohibited Drugs earlier on December 18, 1990.

The WTF Rules and Regulations are composed of 85 Sections in 25 Articles, stating, in its provision of the objects, that Taekwondo is a product of traditional Korean culture. The purpose of organizing the Federation is to propagate and standardize Taekwondo along with its traditional Taekwondo spirit throughout the world and it seeks to achieve an ideal of sports, fast, strongly, and accurately, through Taekwondo competitions.

It is also specified in the Rules and Regulations that the headquarters of the WTF shall be permanently seated in Seoul, Korea, and that the official languages shall be English, French, German, Spanish, and Korean. The WTF officials are the president, 5 vice presidents, a secretary general, a financial commissioner, 19 Executive Council members, and 2 auditors, who all enjoy their 4-year term of office. The general assembly of the WTF will meet biannually.

The WTF also has 4 regional unions as its affiliates, i.e., Asian, African,

Pan-Am, and European Unions. The Executive Council as its assisting organ controls 12 consultative committees, beginning with the Technical Committee and the Refereeing Committee. At present, the WTF has affiliates of over 160 member countries.

Competition Rules

The Competition Rules, which were amended on November 17, 1997, comprise 24 Articles and 75 Sections. A taekwondo contest is conducted on an elastic mat of 12m x 12m wide in 3 rounds of 3 minutes each (3 rounds of 2 minutes for juniors) between two contestants, Blue and Red, and the winner will be decided upon by the system of a quadruple decision-making body, consisting of one referee and 3 judges.

Contestants must wear the competition costume authorized by the WTF, which consists of the taekwondo uniform (dobok) and protection gear, such as trunk protector, head protector, groin guard, and forearm and shin guards. All pieces of protection gear must be carried in hand by each contestant The weights are classified into 8 divisions for Categories Male and Female, respectively (10 weight divisions for juniors, male and female, respectively), and, however, only 4 weight divisions for each category of Mens and Womens are permitted especially for the 2000 Sydney Olympic Games.

The methods of competition are classified into the individual competition and the team competition, the former mainly adopting a tournament system of elimination. Especially for the Olympic Games, a tournament system with a repechage will be adopted for 4 weight divisions, male and female, respectively, to vie for 3 medals, i.e., gold, silver, and bronze, for each weight division. The permitted areas for scoring points are fixed: one on the abdomen of the trunk, two on the flanks, and the face. One scoring gains one point, and the final match score will be the sum of all points scored throughout the 3 rounds. The referee can declare a penalty against any prohibited act. A Gamjeom penalty equals one minus point. Prohibited acts are divided into a Gyeonggo penalty (warning) and a Gamjeom penalty (deduction of point). Three Gamjeoms in a total will bring about a defeat by Referees punitive declaration. Gyeonggo and Gamjeom penalties will be counted cumulatively throughout all 3 rounds.

The decision of the contest results will be a win by KO, by RSC, by score, by withdrawal, by Referees punitive declaration, and others The Referees decision should be absolute and definite, and the Referee should exercise a complete control over all the process of a contest. The judges use electronic scoring instruments linked to a computer system, thereby marking the valid points immediately.

Major International Competitions

The WTF directly sponsors such large events as the World Men's and Women's Taekwondo Championships, the World Male and Female Junior Taekwondo Championships, the World Cup Taekwondo, and others. The 1st World Taekwondo Championships were held in May 1973, the same year of the founding of WTF, and the year 1999 was the 14th World Taekwondo Championships held in Edmonton, Canada. The World Womens Taekwondo Championships was first organized in 1987 in Barcelona, and up to now has recorded its 7th Championships, always accompanying the Mens Championships. As for the World Junior Taekwondo Championships, it has so far registered two times of championships: the 1st in Barcelona in 1996, and the 2nd in Istanbul in September 1998. The World Cup Taekwondo, which was first held in the United States in June 1986, has now registered the 10th of its kind, the last held at Lyons, France, in April 2000.

There are also other international events, namely, the World Collegiate Taekwondo Championships and the CISM Taekwondo Championships, and the Continental Taekwondo Championships sponsored by each of the 4 regional Unions are held every two years. Besides, there are many WTF-recognized international taekwondo tournaments as well as official taekwondo events in multi-sports games, namely, Asian Games, Pan-American Games, SEA Games, All-African Games, South American Games, Central American Sports Games, Central American and Caribbean Games, Bolivarian Sports Games, South Asian Federation Games, South-Pacific Games, or what not.

Internationalization of Taekwondo

The World Taekwondo Federation, which came into existence on May 28, 1973 by the decision of 35 delegates from 19 countries, began to put spurs to the internationalization of taekwondo. Beginning with its affiliation with the General Association of International Sports Federations (GAISF) at the GAISF general meeting held in October 1975 in Montreal, Canada, the WTF managed to make taekwondo adopted as the 23rd official sport of the CISM (International Military Sports Council) in April 1976. Subsequently, in July 1980, the 83rd session of IOC general meeting held in Moscow recognized the WTF as a formal sports organization, which was followed in January 1981 by its affiliation with the ICSSPE (International Council of Sports Science and Physical Education).

In November 1982, the IOC president and the WTF president signed an agreement regarding the assurance of the independence of Olympic movement, which motivated a drive to develop taekwondo into an Olympic sport. Encouraged by all these developments, the WTF could afford to make taekwondo adopted as an official event of the Pan-American Games at the 20th PASO (Pan-American Sports Organization) meeting held in August 1983 in Caracas, and an official event of the All-African Games at a meeting of the Supreme Council of African Sports (SCSA) held in December 1983, which were followed by the WTF affiliation to the IAKS (an international working group on sports and leisure equipment).

Again, in September 1984, the 3rd general meeting of the Olympic

Council of Asia (OCA) adopted taekwondo as an official event of the 1986 Seoul Asian Games. The campaign to make taekwondo an Olympic sport began to shed light in June 1985, when the 90th session of IOC general meeting decided to adopt taekwondo as a demonstration sport for the 24th Seoul Olympic Games 1988. In the meantime, the 7th general assembly of the WTF held in September 1985 in Seoul agreed to found the World Cup Taekwondo. Subsequently, in May 1986, the WTF joined both IOC Fair Play Commission and FISU (International Federation of University Sports).

Taekwondo was also adopted as an official event for the Bolivarian Games at an international conference on South American sports held in February 1986 in Cuenca, and for the South American Games at a meeting of ANOC (Association of National Olympic Committees) in April the same year.

The Southeast Asian Game (SEA Game) and the South Pacific Games also adopted taekwondo as their official event in January and December 1987, respectively.

Taekwondo was adopted for a second time as a demonstration sport of Olympic Games by the IOC general meeting held in April 1989, and participated as such in the 25th Barcelona Olympic Games 1992.

Finally, in February 1995, the ASOIF (Association of International Federations for Summer Olympics) approved taekwondo as its associate event.

The WTF Logo

The logotype of the WTF forms a circle, which contains an inner circle depicting a world globe of ultramarine color, and , at the center of the inner circle, two men pose face-to-face in a side-kick stance.

The rim in between the two circles bears the Korean letters Taekwondo, at the lowest part, and The World Taekwondo Federation in English, covering all the remaining space of the rim. And, the latitudes and longitudes of the globe symbolize 5 Oceans and 6 Continents, which signifies a great leap forward to infiniteness. The globe itself implies a global international sport, representing the World in the denomination of the WTF.

The use of Korean letters and English words implies the native country of taekwondo as well as the official language for its globalization. The circle means taekwondo spirit and solidarity, representing *han* (one) in the *ilyeo* philosophy, i.e., oneness of nature and human being, and oneness of mind and body. Moreover, the ultramarine color signifies the spirit of youthfulness. This logotype was adopted by the inaugural general meeting of the WTF, which was held on May 28, 1973, at Gukgiwon.

Competition Equipment, and Marketing of Their Authorization

The WTF has provided in its Rules and Regulations that all contestants should wear the designated competition equipment including the uniform (dobok), and, therefore, it has been engaged in developing a business of marketing authorized equipment. So far, the authorized items are dobok, mat, scoring instruments and electronic sign board system for competitions, head protector, forearm and shin guards, groin guard, trunk protector, or what not.

Authorized for the first time was the head protector made by Macho Co. in the United States, and by now all the above-listed items are subject to the approval of the WTF for their production. Businesses granted the authorization are Schuram Sports, Adidas, Taekwon Mecca, Grand Master International, IDM Industries, ASL Electronics, and others, which are seated in Germany, Singapore, Korea, Austria, and the United States. Usually the contracts of authorization hold effect for 4 years.

A Home Page on Internet Web

The formal information system of an Internet web home page for the WTF was at first opened on November 1, 1996, with the support of the

DACOM Co. at the Yongsan main office of the company, which was celebrated by the presence of President Son Ik-su and Kang Hak-kyu from the DACOM Co., and President Kim Un-yong, Secretary General Lee Keum-hong, and Deputy Secretary General Lee Kyong-myong from the WTF.

However, the WTF in January 1998 canceled the contract with DACOM regarding the operation-on-commission of the WTF home page. Instead, an affiliated company to GAISF has taken over the running of the home pages covering all sports of International Federations.

The current WTF web-site reads http://www.taekwondo.worldsport. com, and the e-mail address is wtf@unitel.co.kr or office@taekwondo .worldsport.org.

Appendices

Bibliography
Studing Korean Language
Taekwondo Terminology

Bibliography

Chung Yon-jong, *Dangun Invented Hangeul*, Nexus, 1996.

C.A. Vanpeason, Son bong-ho *et al.*, trans., *An Introduction to Philosophical Anthropology*, Seogwangsa, 1985.

D.C. Kofelston, Ahn Jong-su trans., *Philosophy and Culture*, Koreawon, 1994.

D.C. Vanpeason, Son Bong-ho et al., *An Introduction to Philosophical Anthropology,* Seokwangsa, 1985.

Gukgiwon, ed., *National Martial Art Taekwondo Textbook*, Oh Seoung Publishing Co., 1993.

Hwang Jun-yon, *An Understanding of the Korean thoughts*, Pakyongsa, 1995.

Kim Chang-ryong *et al.*, trans., *The Rendezvous of East and West Sports Philosophies*, Bokyongmunhwasa, 1989.

Kim Don, ed., *Hongik-ingan and Handan-gogi*, Yupung Publishing Co., 1995.

Kim Jae-eun, *Psychology of Ki,* Ehwa Womans University Press, 1996.

Kim Sam, *A Survey of Cultural Monuments of Goguryeo*, The Continental Institute Press, 1997.

Kim Sang-il, *The Han Philosophy,* Chonmangsa, 1988.

Kim Sang-il, *The Han Ideology*, Ohnnuri, 1986.

Kim Sang-il, *Theory and Actuality of the Han Ideology*, Chishik-sanopsa, 1990.

Kim Young-hui, trans., *The Body*, Pakyongsa, 1992.

Koh Young-dong, *The History of Ancient Korean Martial Arts*, Hanppuri, 1993.

Korea National Ethics Society, ed., *The Traditional Thoughts of Korea*, Hyongsol Publishing Co., 1996.

Korean Cultural Corporate Identity Dictionary Compiling Committee, *A Dictionary of Korean Cultural, Symbols*, Dong-A Publishing Co., 1994.

Lee Jung-jae, *The Philosophical Thoughts of the Universe in the Korean Race*, Myongmundang, 1993.

Lee Kyong-myong, *Dynamic Taekwondo,* Hollym, 1995

Lee Kyong-myong, *Taekwondo,* Daewonsa, 1997

Park Chan-hui, *The Somato-kinetics of Sports*, Sejong Publishing Co., 1993.

Science and Philosophy Research Association, *Science and Philosophy* Vol. 4, Tongnamu, 1993.

The Haedong Society of Philosophy, *A Study on the Korean Philosophy*, Vol. 21, 1992.

The World Taekwondo Federation, *Taekwondo Handbook*, 1996.

The Yongnam Society of Philosophy, *Series of Treatises on Philosophy* Vol. 3, 1987.

Studing Korean Language

Ⅰ. BASIC

1. Vowels(모음)

Korean vowels are named phonetically.

vowels	아	야	어	여	오	요	우	유	으	이
pronunciation	[a]	[ja]	[ə]	[jə]	[o]	[jo]	[u]	[ju]	[ɨ]	[i]
korean words	아	야	어	여	오	요	우	유	으	이

⊙ The order of writing

The order of writing is from top to bottom and from left to right.

야 → ㅇ 이 아 야
요 → ㅇ ㅇ ㅇ 요

아이	오이	아우	여유
여우	이유	우유	야유

2. Consonants(자음)

The names and sounds of Korean consonants are as following.

consonants	ㄱ	ㄴ	ㄷ	ㄹ	ㅁ	ㅂ	ㅅ
pronunciation	[k]	[n]	[t]	[l]	[m]	[p]	[s]
korean words	기역	니은	디귿	리을	미음	비읍	시옷
consonants	ㅇ	ㅈ	ㅊ	ㅋ	ㅌ	ㅍ	ㅎ
pronunciation	[ŋ]	[c]	[ch]	[kh]	[th]	[ph]	[h]
korean words	이응	지읒	치읓	키읔	티읕	피읖	히읗

⊙ The order of writing

ㄱ →   ㄴ →   ㄷ →   ㄹ →   ㅁ →

ㅂ →   ㅅ →   ㅇ →   ㅈ →   ㅊ →

ㅋ →   ㅌ →   ㅍ →   ㅎ →

가게	나이	구두	다리
머리	바지	소리	자리
차리다	코	타다	파리

3. Table of Korean Syllables(한국어 음절표)

Vowels Consonants	ㅏ	ㅑ	ㅓ	ㅕ	ㅗ	ㅛ	ㅜ	ㅠ	ㅡ	ㅣ
ㄱ	가	갸	거	겨	고	교	구	규	그	기
ㄴ	나	냐	너	녀	노	뇨	누	뉴	느	니
ㄷ	다	댜	더	뎌	도	됴	두	듀	드	디
ㄹ	라	랴	러	려	로	료	루	류	르	리
ㅁ	마	먀	머	며	모	묘	무	뮤	므	미
ㅂ	바	뱌	버	벼	보	뵤	부	뷰	브	비
ㅅ	사	샤	서	셔	소	쇼	수	슈	스	시
ㅇ	아	야	어	여	오	요	우	유	으	이
ㅈ	자	쟈	저	져	조	죠	주	쥬	즈	지
ㅊ	차	챠	처	쳐	초	쵸	추	츄	츠	치
ㅋ	카	캬	커	켜	코	쿄	쿠	큐	크	키
ㅌ	타	탸	터	텨	토	툐	투	튜	트	티
ㅍ	파	퍄	퍼	펴	포	툐	푸	퓨	프	피
ㅎ	하	햐	허	혀	호	효	후	휴	흐	히

4. Some Single Vowels and Dipthong

Besides 10 basic vowels mentioned before, there are another 11 vowels.

모 음	애	얘	에	예	와	왜
소 리	[ɛ]	[i ɛ]	[e]	[je]	[wa]	[wɛ]

모 음	외	워	웨	위	의	
소 리	[ɸ]	[w ə]	[we]	[wi]	[i i]	

◎ The Ordering of writing

예 → ㅇ 이 야 예   왜 → ㅇ 오 외 왜
웨 → ㅇ 우 위 웨   의 → ㅇ 으 의

    애기   얘기   에서   예사
    왜   외우다   위   의자

5. Double Consonants(쌍자음)

자 음	ㄲ	ㄸ	ㅃ	ㅆ	ㅉ
이 름	쌍기역	쌍디귿	쌍비읍	쌍시옷	쌍지읒
음 가	[k']	[t']	[p']	[s']	[c']

    꾸다   꼬리
    딸   띠
    빠르다   뿌리
    쌀   씨
    짜다   쪼다

6. Corresponding Sounds in English(이 소리와 닮았어요)

Vowels	ㅏ as in f<u>a</u>ther	ㅒ as in <u>y</u>ale
	ㅑ as in <u>y</u>ard, <u>y</u>ah	ㅔ as in P<u>e</u>n, s<u>e</u>nd
	ㅓ as in c<u>o</u>mputer	ㅖ as in <u>y</u>e<u>ll</u>ow
	ㅕ as in <u>y</u>earn	ㅘ as in <u>wh</u>at, <u>w</u>atch
	ㅗ as in f<u>o</u>rth, board	ㅙ as in <u>we</u>lcome
	ㅛ as in y<u>o</u>gi	ㅚ as in <u>wa</u>ft, <u>wa</u>ff
	ㅜ as in g<u>oo</u>d, b<u>oo</u>t	ㅝ as in <u>wa</u>r, <u>wa</u>rm
	ㅠ as in f<u>ew</u>, <u>u</u>se	ㅞ as in <u>swea</u>ter
	ㅡ as in thr<u>ough</u>	ㅟ as in w<u>ee</u>k, win
	ㅣ as in m<u>ee</u>t, s<u>i</u>t	ㅢ (no corresponding sound in English)
	ㅐ as in f<u>a</u>t, c<u>a</u>t	
Consonants	ㄱ as in Kim, again	ㅌ as in <u>t</u>ea, <u>t</u>eacher
	ㄴ as in <u>n</u>ose, <u>n</u>et, soo<u>n</u>	ㅍ as in <u>p</u>eople, <u>p</u>ork
	ㄷ as in <u>t</u>one, a<u>d</u>opt	ㅎ as in <u>h</u>orse, <u>h</u>ome
	ㄹ as in <u>l</u>ion	ㄲ as in gossip
	ㅁ as in <u>m</u>other, co<u>m</u>e	(q sound in Spanish)
	ㅂ as in <u>p</u>ony, a<u>b</u>out	ㄸ as in s<u>t</u>op
	ㅅ as in <u>s</u>mile	(t sound in Spanish)
	ㅇ as in you<u>ng</u>	ㅃ as in s<u>p</u>eak, s<u>p</u>eed
	ㅈ as in gara<u>g</u>e	(p sound in Spanish)
	ㅊ as in <u>ch</u>arge, <u>ch</u>ance	ㅆ as in <u>s</u>ick, <u>s</u>elf
	ㅋ as in <u>c</u>reate, <u>c</u>rown	ㅉ as in <u>J</u>ack

Vowels and consonants sounds that English does not have, We noted with the most similar sounds in English. And note that some vowels have the same sound through the historical change. ex. ㅐ' and ㅔ', 'ㅙ' and 'ㅚ'

7. Final Consonant's Sound(받침소리)

All the consonants may come at the end of the syllables, but only 7 consonants as ㄱ, ㄴ, ㄷ, ㄹ, ㅁ, ㅂ, ㅅ, ㅇ have phonetic sounds. But when the final consonant sounds have liaison with vowels of other syllables, you pronounce it phonetically.

Final consonant's sound

ㄱ ㄲ ㅋ	ㄴ	ㄷ ㅌ ㅅ ㅆ ㅈ ㅎ	ㄹ	ㅁ	ㅂ ㅍ	ㅇ
[k]	[n]	[t]	[l]	[m]	[p]	[ŋ]

달	책상	부엌
돈	다섯	앞에서
집안	영어	믿어요

8. Double Consonants(겹받침)

When the double consonants come at the the end of syllable sometimes you pronounce the first consonant sometimes the second.

받침	ㄳ	ㄵ	ㄶ	ㄻ	ㄽ	ㄾ	ㄿ	ㅄ	ㄺ	ㄺ
소리값	[k]	[n]	[n]	[m]	[l]	[l]	[p]	[p]	[l,p]	[l,k]

몫   앉다   많다   젊다
곳   핥다   읊   없다

넓다 [nəlt'a]   밟다 [papt'a]
맑게 [malk'e]   맑다 [makt'a]

II. GRAMMAR(문법)

1. -이다/입니다.

'-이다' is used to finish sentences after noun stems.

'-입니다' is a honorific expression of '-이다'.

사람   나는 사람<u>이다</u>.   나는 사람<u>입니다</u>.

사과   이것은 사과<u>이다</u>.   이것은 사과<u>입니다</u>.

책   이것은 책<u>이다</u>.   이것은 책<u>입니다</u>.

2. -ㅂ니다/습니다.

The sentence endings '-ㅂ니다/습니다' are used in order to express the polite style of address. The ending '-ㅂ니다' comes after verb stems ending in vowels. And '-습니다' comes after verb stems ending in consonants. Look at the following examples.

보 + 다 - 보 +

(stem) (ending)   ㅂ니다 → 봅니다.

모음으로 끝남

오 + 다 - 오 +

      ㅂ니다 → 옵니다.

먹 + 다 - 먹 +

(stem) (ending) 습니다 → 먹습니다.

자음으로 끝남

있 + 다 - 있 +

습니다 → 있습니다.

3. -ㅂ니까?/습니까?

The sentence endings '-ㅂ니까?/습니까?' are used in order to express the polite style of inquiry. The same rules as '-ㅂ니다/습니다' can be applied to '-ㅂ니까?/습니까?'

보 + 다 - 보 +

ㅂ니까? → 봅니까?

가 + 다 - 가 +

ㅂ니까? → 갑니까?

읽 + 다 - 읽 +

습니까? → 읽습니까?

좋 + 다 - 좋 +

습니까? → 좋습니까?

4. -은/-는

'-은/-는' are used as topic particles at the subject position in sentences. These particles are used to indicate the constrast between topics and to put an emphasis on topics.

나 + 는 → 나는

학생 + 은 → 학생은

5. Korean Sentences

English sentences are constructed like this sequence Subject + Verb +

Object. Korean sectences are however constructed like this sequence <u>Subject + Object + Verb.</u> The most important factor in Korean is the predicate.

주어 + 목적어 + 서술어(동사)
subject   object   predicative verb
학생이   책을   읽습니다.

6. -이/-가

The topic particles '-이/-가' are attached to subject nouns or pronouns. If nouns end in consonants. the topic particle '-이' is used as a subject particle ; if nouns end in vowels, the topic particle '-가' is used as a subject particle.

이것   이것 + <u>이</u>   →   이것이
         이름 + <u>이</u>   →   이름이

내   내 + <u>가</u>   →   내가
       친구 + <u>가</u>   →   친구가

7. 안

These negative words '안' are used in front of verbs, adjectives, and predicative particles to express negation. They are found in Various types of sentences such as declarative, interrogative, promising sentences.

하다   안   하다
만나다   안   만나다

우유를 안 마십니다.
그를 안 만납니다.
오늘은 비가 안 옵니다.

8. 나/너/저

The first personal pronoun '나' is used to indicate one speaker himself. This (나) is a common form to refer to a speaker. '내', the alternative form of '나' is matched with only a subject particle '가'.

The second personal pronoun '너' is a common form which is used for a speaker to indicate his or her interlocutor when the speakers are of the same age or friends. '네', the alternative form of '너', is matched with only a subject particle '가'. Similarly with '내', '네' is different from the contracted form '네' from '너의' which means 'possessive'.

There is another first personal pronoun '저'. This pronoun shows the polite attitude of the speakers. This is usually used when the speaker is younger then the interlocutor. '제', the alternative form of '저' is used together with only a subject particle '-가',

9. 누구/누가

The interrogative pronouns '누가' and '누구' are used to indicate questions about people.

저 사람이 <u>누구냐?</u>
<u>누구를</u> 만납니까?
<u>누가</u> 노래를 잘합니까?

10. 분

The subordinate pronoun '분' is used to indicate each person. It means 'person' and '분' expresses speakers polite attitude rather than '사람'. This pronoun should always be used together with indicative adjectives '이, 그, 저' in front of '분'.

11. -아요/-어요

The sentence endings '-아요/-어요' are used to express informal polite style of adress. The ending '-아요' is attached to verb stems ending in vowels ; the ending '-어요' is attached to verb stems ending in consonants.

12. -(으)세요

'-(으)세요' is a honorific expression of '-아요/-어요'.
This form express a declarative, a question, an imperative depending on speaker's intonation.

많이 잡수세요.
어서 오세요.

13. 여기/저기/거기

These pronouns '여기/저기/거기' are used to indicate the place. '여기' means 'here' which indicates the place where the speakers and hearers are staying. '저기' means 'over there' which indicates the place where the speakers and hearers are away from. '거기' means 'there' which indicates the place where the hearers are staying. Or '거기' indicates other places that the speakers and hearers are supposed to be aware of.

14. -와/-과

The conjunctive words '-와/-과' are used to combine two nouns. When the former nouns end in consonants, the speakers use '-과' ; when the former nouns end in vowels, the speakers use '-와'.

사과 + 와
책상 + 과

15. 숫자

1	2	3	4	5	6	7	8	9	10
하나	둘	셋	넷	다섯	여섯	일곱	여덟	아홉	열
일	이	삼	사	오	육	칠	팔	구	십

10	20	30	40	50	60	70	80	90	100
열	스물	서른	마흔	쉰	예순	일흔	여든	아흔	백
십	이십	삼십	사십	오십	육십	칠십	팔십	구십	백

16. 몇

This interrogative word '몇' is used to ask a specific time.

몇 사람이에요?
사과를 몇 개나 샀습니까?
지금 몇 시입니까?
몇 시에 만날까요?
모임이 몇 시에 있습니까?

17. -에서

The locative particle '-에서' appears after locative nouns and express the place where something is happening.
The locative particle '-에서' indicates starting points.

저는 부산에서 삽니다.
어디에서 일하십니까?
시장에서 바지를 샀습니다.
도서관에서 책을 봅니다.
나는 방에서 음악을 듣습니다.

어디에서 오셨습니까?

저는 미국에서 왔습니다.

몇 시에 회사에서 출발합니까?

부산에서 전화가 왔습니다.

18. -하고

This conjunctive particle '-하고' serves as a conjunction similar with '-와/-과'. '-하고' combines two nouns.

교실에 선생님하고 학생이 있습니다.

엄마하고 아기가 잠을 잡니다.

19. -에 있다/없다

The locative particle '-에' is attached to nouns to indicate the place where things are. This locative particle '에' is used together with the following predicatives '있다, 없다' which refer to the existence, nonexistence respectively. However, when the speakers are going to mention the existence or the non-existence of people and to express polite style, then use the honorific forms '계시다, 계시지 않다'.

20. 위치(location)

위(on,above,over) 오른쪽(right side)

아래, 밑(under) 왼쪽(left side)

앞(front) 안, 속(left side)

뒤(back) 밖, 겉(outside)

옆(next,by,beside)

21. -았-/-었-/-였-

The tense particles '-았-/-었-/-였-' show the speakers intention or supposition, or the completion or progress of evets. They are attached to verb stems. If the verb stems end in '오' or '아', '었' is attached to the verb stems. If the verb stems end in '하-', '-였-' is attached to verb stems.

(1) '-았-'
ㅏ+았   가+았+다 - 가았다(가았습니다) - 갔다(갔습니다)
ㅗ+았   오+았+다 - 오았다(오았습니다) - 왔다(왔습니다)
ㅗ+았   보+았+다 - 보았다(보았습니다) - 봤다(봤습니다)

(2) '-었-'
ㅓ+었   먹+었+다 - 먹었다(먹었습니다)
ㅓ+었   서+었+다 - 서었다(서었습니다) - 섰다(섰습니다)
ㅡ+었   쓰+었+다 - 쓰었다(쓰었습니다) - 썼다(썼습니다)
ㅜ+었   배우+었+다 - 배우었다(배우었습니다) - 배웠다(배웠습니다)

(3) '-였-'
하+였, 하다-하였다(하였습니다) - 했다(했습니다)
        공부하다-공부하였다-공부했다(공부했습니다)

22. -도

The additive particle '-도' can appear after nouns. It indicates the common things with other things or the same class with other things. It is also used to show an emphasis.

그분은 한국 사람입니다. 저도 한국 사람입니다.
그 사람은 학생도 아니고 선생님도 아니에요.

23. 그런데

The conjunctive word '그런데' is used when the speakers are going to tell the interlocutors contrasting or prrosite things. The another use is for changing topics or supplementing explanation.

24. -시-

The honorific '-시-' can be inserted into predicative words. If verb stems end in vowels, '-시-' is inserted ; if the verb stems end in consonants, '-으시' is inserted into predicative words.

선생님이 오시었다.
아버지는 일을 하십니다.

25. 시/분/초(time expressions)

The word '시' is used for the hour : Korean cardinal numbers are used in front of '시'. The word '분' is used for the minute ; Mandarine numbers are used in front of '분'. The word '초' is used for the second ; Mandarine numbers are used in front of '초'.

1 : 01 - 한 시 일 분   10 : 48 - 열 시 사십 팔 분
2 : 05 - 두 시 오 분   11 : 24 - 열한 시 이십 사 분
3 : 15 - 세 시 십오 분   12 : 00 - 열두 시
4 : 30 - 네 시 삼십 분
5 : 45 - 다섯 시 사십 오 분
6 : 53 - 여섯 시 오십 삼 분

26. 무엇(무엇, 무어, 뭐)

The interrogative pronoun '무엇' is used to indicate questions about things but not people. This word '무엇' can have changes morphologically like '뭐' or '무어'. '뭐' together with subject particle '가' are used as subjects in sectences.

이것이 무엇입니까?

교실에 무엇이 있습니까?

너는 무엇을 하니?

뭐 + 가 → 뭐가(주격)

뭐 + ㄹ → 뭘(목적격)

방에 뭐가 있습니까?

너는 뭘 하니?

27. -지 않다(-지 않습니다)

The negative predicative '-지 않다' is attached to verbal or adjective stems to express negative meaning

요즘은 바쁘지 않습니다.

영수가 숙제를 하지 않습니다.

28. -고 싶다

This ending '-고 싶다' is used to express the speaker's intention. This ending is used with the first personal nouns is the declarative sentences. This ending is used with the second personal nouns in the interrogative sectences. This ending is transformed into '-고 싶어하다' when it is used with the third personal pronouns.

제주도에 가고 싶다.

나는 지금 자고 싶다.

너도 학교 가고 싶니?

29. -(으)려고 하다

This ending '-려고 하다' is attached to the active verb stems to express plans or intention of the subjuct. When the verb stems end in vowels. '-려고 하다' is attached to verb stems. When the verb stems end in consonants. '-으려고 하다' is attachend to the verb stems.

30. -(으)ㄴ/는

These are modifier endings which attach to a verb stem and serve to modify a following noun.

Vstem + (으)ㄴ/는

좋 + 은 → 좋은 책(N)

(자음으로 끝나는 형용사 + 은)

기쁘 + ㄴ → 기쁜 얼굴(N)

(모음으로 끝나는 형용사 + ㄴ)

먹 + 는 → 먹는 사람(N)

(동사 + 는)

가 + 는 → 가는 길(N)

(동사 + 는)

31. -에 얼마

This interrogative word '얼마' follows the particle '-에', which are used after numbers or time to indicate the strandard for value.

그것은 한 개에 얼마입니까?

파 한 단에 얼마예요?

일주일에 얼마를 받아요?

32. -게

This particle '-게' is attached to the verb stems and functions as an adverb.

한국말을 쉽 + 게 배웁니다.

아침에 늦 + 게 일어났어요.

33. -아/-어 보다

These particles '-아/-어' are used to indicate the trial of the main verbs and the checking the results of the main verbs.

가다   가 + 보다   가 보세요.
먹다   먹어 + 보다   먹어 보세요.

34. -ㄹ까요?

This ending is used to indicate the speaker's doubt or supposition. The ending '-ㄹ까요' is attached to the verb stems ending in vowels ; the ending '을까요' is attached to the verb stems ending in consonants.

(같이)   가 + ㄹ까요 → 갈까요?
(내일)   만나 + ㄹ까요 → 만날까요?

35. -(으)ㅂ시다

The ending '-ㅂ시다' is attached to the verb stems to show the polite attitude for the speakers to suggest or offer doing somethings. When the verb stems end in vowels, the ending '-ㅂ시다' is attached consonants, '-읍시다' is attached to the verb stems.

가다 - 가+ㅂ시다 - 갑시다
공부하다 - 공부하+ㅂ시다-공부합시다
앉다 - 앉+읍시다-앉읍시다
먹다 - 먹+읍시다-먹읍시다

36. -(으)십시오

The ending '-(으)십시오' is used in the polite command sentence. This ending is always attached to the action verbs.

책을 읽 + 으십시오

이 돈을 받 + 으십시오

안녕히 가 + 십시오

맛있게 드 + 십시오

37. -지 말다

This ending '-지 말다' is attached to the verb stems to form negative commands and negative suggestions in the commanding or recommending sentences.

명령형	먹 + 지 말아라	→	먹지 말아라
	가 + 지 말아라	→	가지 말아라
권유형	먹 + 지 마십시오	→	먹지 마십시오
	가 + 지 마십시오	→	가지 마십시오

38. -겠-

'-겠-' is inserted between verb stems and sentence endings to indicate the speakers intention or plan. This infix is used with the first or second personal pronouns. This infix '-겠-' together with honorifics such as '-으시-' is used to express the speakers' polite attitede.

39. -(으)로

The ending '-(으)로' is attached to locative nouns to indicate the direction. The locative ending '-에' can be confused with the directive particle '-(으)로', letter is used to show the direction.

어디로 가십니까?

이쪽으로 오십시오.

40. -(으)러 가다

This ending '-(으)러 가다' is attached to the verb stems to deliver direct objects or intention in doing activities.

영화를 보 + 러 　　 갈까요
수영을 하 + 러 　　 갑니다
밥을 먹 + 으러 　　 갑니다

41. 못

The negative word '못' has an inherent meaning 'can't. This is usually used with verbs ; this is rarely found in the negation of adjectives. And it can't be used in promising sentences, either.

42. -기 때문에

This ending '-기 때문에' is used to indicate the reason or cause for the following actions.

오늘은 수업이 없다. 집에서 쉰다.

↓

+ 기 때문에

→ 오늘은 수업이 없기 때문에 집에서 쉰다.

43. ㅂ 불규칙 동사

If the verb stems end in Korean consonant 'ㅂ', and if those verb stems are attached to the particles or endings beginning with vowels, 'ㄴ/ㅁ', and 'ㅅ' then the final consonant 'ㅂ' of the verb stems is deleted and the vowel 'ㅜ' is added to the verb stems. However, if the verbs '곱다, 돕다' are attached to the ending '-어요', the vowel 'ㅗ' is added instead of the vowel 'ㅜ'.

	춥다			아름답다	

추우 + 어요 → 추워요   아름다우 + 어요 → 아름다워요

춥	+	게	아름답	+	게
춥	+	고	아름답	+	고
추우	+	면	아름다우	+	면
추우	+	니	아름다우	+	니
추우	+	ㄴ	아름다우	+	ㄴ

44. -아/-어 서

The ending '-아서' is attached to the verb stems and accompanies another verb. So this ending '-아서' combine two verbs to indicate the procedual process of two actions.

And it indicates that the action of the clause is the reason for the action of the second clause.

식당에 가(다) + 서 점심을 먹습니다.
친구를 만나(다) + 서 학교에 갔어요
여기에 앉(다) + 아서 기다리세요

45. ㄹ 불규칙 동사

If the verb stems end in Korean consonant 'ㄹ', and if those verb stems are attached to the particles or endings which are starting with Korean consonant 'ㄴ, ㅂ, ㅅ', then the final consonant 'ㄹ' of the verb stems is deleted.

46. -에 서 ~ -까지

The alternative forms of point particles '-부터, -까지' are '-에서, -까지' which can be used in the same situation.

여기 + 서   거기 + 까지는 몇 킬로미터에요?
부산 + 에서   서울 + 까지 기차로 왔어요.

47. -부터/까지

The particle '-부터' is used to indicate temporal starting points ; the particle '-까지' is used to indicate the spacious temporal ending points.

여기 + 부터 주세요   서울역 + 까지 갑니다
9시 + 부터 시작합니다   세시   + 까지 기다렸어요
오늘 + 부터 일하세요   병   + 까지 생겼어요

48. -(으)ㄹ

This ending '-(으)ㄹ' is used to indicate the speaker's intention or aim after verbs. This modifies a following noun.

하 + ㄹ   일(N)
입 + 을   옷(N)
친구를 만날 생각입니다.
토요일에 소풍을 갈 겁니다.

49. -고

The conjunctive particle '-고' functions as a conjunction combining two coordinate clauses. These two clauses can be placed in reverse order without the differences of meaning.

This particle '-고' can be used to indicate contrastion facts between two things.

This particle '-고' can be used to combine two verbs which show the sequence of changes.

(1) 하늘은 푸르고 물은 맑다.
    그는 학자이고 정치가이다.
    이건 삼백 원이고 저건 사백 원입니다.
(2) 길고 짧은 것.
    A는 키가 크고 B는 작다.
(3) 나는 손을 씻고 밥을 먹는다.
    형은 학교에 가고 동생은 극장에 가요.

50. -(으)ㄹ 수 있다/없다

This form attaches to verb stems to indicate ability or possibility. If the verb stem ends in a vowel, use '-ㄹ 수 있다'. If the verb stem ends is a consonant, use '-을 수 있다', '-(으)ㄹ 수 없다' is a negative of this expression.

한국말을 잘 할 수 있습니다.
신문을 읽을 수 있습니다.
김치를 먹을 수 없습니다.
내일 만날 수 없습니다.

51. -게 되다

This ending '-게 되다' is attached to verb stems to describe the change or development of some states.

한국말을 잘하게 되었습니다.
김치를 좋아하게 되었습니다.
부산에 살게 되었습니다.

52. 아직

This adverb '아직' is used in the negative sentence to mean the incomplete stata of the situation or action.

김 선생님이 아직 오지 않았어요.

그 숙제를 아직 못 했어요.

점심을 아직 안 먹었어요.

53. -(으)면 안돼요?

This ending '-(으)면 안돼요?' is attached to the verb stems to indicate that the speaker is trying to persuade the hearer to change his/her mind or intention.

내일 다시 오면 안돼요?

지금 텔레비전 보면 안돼요?

54. -기 전에

This particle '-기 전에' is attached to the verb stems. This combines two actions which are taking place in order. The action in front of this particle happens after the other action.

한국에 오기 전에 미국에 살았어요.

식사하기 전에 손을 씻으세요.

수업이 끝나기 전에 오세요.

55. -(으)ㄴ 후에

This particle '-(으)ㄴ 후에' is attached to the verb stems. This combines two actions which are taking place in order. The action in front of this particle happens before the other action.

저녁을 먹은 후에 편지를 썼어요.

한국말을 배운 후에 한국에서 일하겠어요.

수업이 끝난 후에 뭐해요?

56. Reading(읽기)

Writting letters

어머니께

그동안 안녕하셨어요? 저도 건강하게 잘 있습니다.

이곳에 와보니 집생각이 더 납니다.

식구들이 많이 보고 싶습니다. 개구쟁이 동생도 잘 있겠지요.

저는 이곳에서 한국어도 배우고 여행도 하면서 지내고 있습니다.

이곳은 날씨도 좋고, 사람들도 모두 예의바르며 친절합니다.

어제는 백화점에 가서 식구들 선물을 샀습니다. 그런데, 비싸서

많이 못 샀어요. 이제 며칠 있으면 집에 돌아갑니다.

가서 재미있는 얘기, 많이 해드릴게요.

그때까지 안녕히 계세요.

년 월 일

영수 올림

Taekwondo Terminology

한글/Korean	발음/Pronunciation	영어/English
관장님	Gwanjang-nim	President/Grand Master
사범님	Sabeom-nim	Master
조교님	Jogyo-nim	Assistant
선배	Seonbae	Senior
후배	Hubae	Junior
수련생	Suryeonsaeng	Students
유단자	Yudanja	Black Belt Holder
초보자	Choboja	Beginner
체육관	Cheyukgwan	Gumnasium
태권도 정신	Taekwondo Jeongsin	The spirit of Taekwondo
관원 선서	Gwanwon Seonseo	The Student's Oath
체육관 규칙	Cheyukgwan Gyuchik	Rules of the Gymnasium
승급 심사	Seunggeub Simsa	Promotion Test
묵념	Muknyeom	Meditation/Tribute
국기에 대한 경례	Gukgie Daehan Gyeongnye	Salute the National Flag
도복	Dobok	Taekwondo uniform
경례	Gyeongnye	Bow
반대	Bandae	Reverse
왼쪽	Oen Jjok	Left
오른쪽	Oreun Jjok	Right
앞	Ap	Front
뒤	Dwi	Back
준비 운동	Junbi Undong	Warming up
기본	Gibon	Basic
기본 자세	Gibon Jase	Basic Stance
기본 동작	Gibon Dongjak	Basic Movement
기술	Gisul	Technique
호신술	Hosinsul	Self Defense
격파	Gyeokpa	Breaking
시범	Sibeom	Demonstration
급소	Geupso	Vital Points
차렷	Charyeot	Attention
쉬어	Swieo	At ease
준비	Junbi	Ready
시작	Sijak	Start(Begin)
바로	Baro	Stop
갈려	Gallyeo	Break

한글/Korean	발음/Pronunciation	영어/English
계속	Gyesok	Continue
그만	Geuman	End
얼굴	Eolgul	Face(High Section)
몸통	Momtong	Trunk(Middle Section)
아래	Arae	Low Section
품새	Pumsae	Form(Pattern)
겨루기	Gyeorugi	Sparring
한번겨루기	Hanbeon Gyeorugi	One Step Sparring
맞추어 겨루기	Machueo Gyeorugi	Pre-arranged Sparring
주먹	Jumeok	Fist
등주먹	Deungjumeok	Back Fist
메주먹	Mejumeok	Hammer Fist
편주먹	Pyeonjumeok	Flat Fist
밤주먹	Bamjumeok	Chestnut Fist
집게주먹	Jipgejumeok	Pincers Fist
손날	Sonnal	Hand Knife (Hand Blade)
손날등	Sonnaldeung	Reverse Hand Knife
손끝	Sonkkeut	Spear Finger (Fingertips)
가위손끝	Gawisonkkeut	Scissors Spear Fingertips
한손끝	Hansonkkeut	Single Spear Fingertip
아금손	Ageumson	Arc Hand
바탕손	Batangson	Palm Fist
바깥팔목	Bakkat palmok	Outer Wrist
안팔목	Anpalmok	Inner Wrist
등팔목	Deungpalmok	Back Wrist
밑팔목	Mitpalmok	Underside Wrist
팔굽	Palgup	Elbow
앞축	Apchuk	Front Sole
뒤축	Dwitchuk	Back Sole
발날	Balnal	Knife Foot
발바닥	Balbadak	Inside Foot
발등	Baldeung	Instep
뒤꿈치	Dwikkumchi	Heel
발끝	Balkkeut	Toes
무릎	Mureup	Knee